Poems 1953–1983

By the same author

Poems
Home Truths
The Owl in the Tree
The Stones of Emptiness
Penguin Modern Poets 18 (with A. Alvarez and Roy Fuller)
Inscriptions
New Confessions
A Portion for Foxes
Victorian Voices

Criticism
Contemporary English Poetry: an Introduction
Poetry Today, 1960–1973
Twentieth-Century English Poetry
Six Centuries of Verse

For Children
Beyond the Inhabited World: Roman Britain

Travel and Topography
The Deserts of Hesperides
Japan (with Roloff Beny)
In Italy (with Roloff Beny and Peter Porter)
Odyssey: Mirror of the Mediterranean (with Roloff Beny)

As Editor
New Poems 1961 (with Hilary Corke and William Plomer)
Penguin Book of Japanese Verse (with Geoffrey Bownas)
The English Poets (with Peter Porter)
New Poetry 4 (with Fleur Adcock)
Larkin at Sixty
Poetry 1945 to 1980 (with John Mole)
The Gregory Awards Anthology 1981 and 1982 (with Howard Sergeant)

Poems 1953–1983

Anthony Thwaite

Secker & Warburg · London

First published in England 1984 by
Martin Secker & Warburg Limited
54 Poland Street, London W1V 3DF

Copyright © Anthony Thwaite 1984

British Library Cataloguing in Publication Data

Thwaite, Anthony
 Poems 1953–1983
 I. Title
 821'.914[F]   PR6070.H/

ISBN 0-436-52151-2

SUBSIDISED BY THE
Arts Council
OF GREAT BRITAIN

Printed in Great Britain by Redwood Burn Ltd, Trowbridge

For Ann

Preface

This collection draws on seven books, beginning with *Home Truths* (1957). I am grateful to the Marvell Press for permission to reprint eight of the forty poems from that first book. To give the proportions in this way may, however, suggest a misleading notion of *Poems 1953–1983*. Reading through well over three hundred poems I have published during the past thirty years, I spent part of the summer of 1983 in varying moods of depression, exasperation and, infrequently, satisfaction. It would not be true to say, in the traditional form of words, that this book contains 'all that the author wishes to preserve'. For example, if my book *New Confessions* deserves to be read at all, it should be read as a whole. The four sections (out of fifty) printed here were chosen because I think they stand some chance of being sensibly read out of context: to have included the whole sequence would have made the present book too unwieldy and too expensive. Only one book, *Victorian Voices*, is given in full – though, as with *New Confessions*, I have omitted the notes it originally carried.

The book ends with twenty-one poems, hitherto uncollected, written since *A Portion for Foxes* and *Victorian Voices* were completed. Several of these were broadcast by the BBC, and several appeared in the following journals and anthologies: *Listener, London Review of Books, New Poems 1978, New Poems 1982, New Poems 3, New Statesman, Poetry Book Society Supplements 1980 and 1981, Poetry Review, Quarto, The Third Dimension, Three, The Times Literary Supplement, Vole*.

In putting together the collection, the only revisions I have made have been in the way of correcting perpetuated misprints in earlier books, and of changing, adding or omitting the odd word in a handful of poems. A close friend urged me to follow the principle of 'What I have written I have written', and to make this a full-scale Collected Poems. Others advised a stringency which would have resulted in a possibly trim but also possibly meagre Selected Poems. I have decided on a middle course, substantially including the contents of five of the six books published by Oxford University Press between 1963 and 1980, and about half of the uncollected poems on which I could draw. Others will say whether there is too little, or too much.

Contents

from *Inscriptions* (1973)

from *New Confessions* (1974)

from *A Portion for Foxes* (1977)

Victorian Voices (1980)

Uncollected Poems

from *Home Truths*

1 Oedipus

If she who first embodied me
From swollen foetus crouched beneath
Hot sallow blood and milk, if she
Speaks through your eyes, tastes of your breath,
Then hide me where I cannot see.

For when you spoke, it was her face
Which looked through mists of flesh and age
And saw a child. In your embrace
I trudged a lifetime's pilgrimage
From prince's birth to king's disgrace.

I snuggle in your belly: you
Who banish all love's doubts but this
Can never see what sickness grew
Under the sweet drug of your kiss,
Who buckled on a cripple's shoe.

Held fast against your breast, I find
A shapeless memory takes shape
Upon the pillow. Heart and mind
Blunt both my eyes in blind escape
And when I waken, I am blind.

2 The Silent Woman

Take whatever just reward
Is yours to take and yours to keep,
Drag your bench to the full board;
Eat; drink; and after, sleep.
My house is yours, bread, milk and bed.
You have what flesh has coveted.

Do not ask me why I give
Shelter to no one else but you.
Hooded in silence, let us live
Without a thought of lodgers who
Shared the cup where now your lip
Sours the drink at which you sip.

And do not ask me what I see
When, waking from a frowning dream,
Your heavy eyes uncover me
Knotting the sheets until they seem
Horned like a dragon, in whose lair
You've woken, drowsy with despair.

For if you asked, what answer could
Square truth with fable, love with lies?
History like this can do no good
To you, who have no memories,
No raven heart which hoards away
Sour milk, soiled sheets, of yesterday.

3   *Death of a Rat*

Nothing the critic said of tragedy,
Groomed for the stage and mastered into art,
Was relevant to this; yet I could see
Pity and terror mixed in equal part.
Dramatically, a farce right from the start,
Armed with a stick, a hairbrush and a broom,
Two frightened maladroits shut in one room.

Convenient symbol for a modern hell,
The long lean devil and the short squat man
No doubt in this were psychological,
Parable for the times, Hyperion
And Satyr, opposites in union . . .
Or Lawrence's *Snake*, to turn the picture round –
Man's pettiness by petty instinct bound.

But, to be honest, it was neither, and
That ninety minutes skirring in a duel
Was nothing if not honest. The demand
Moved him towards death, and me to play the fool,
Yet each in earnest. I went back to school
To con the hero's part, who, clung with sweat,
Learned where the hero, fool and coward met.

Curtain to bed and bed to corner, he
Nosed at each barrier, chattered, crouched, and then
Eluded me, till art and fear and pity
Offered him to me at the moment when
I broke his back, and smashed again, again,
Primitive, yes, exultant, yes, and knowing
His eyes were bright with some instinctive thing.

If every violent death is tragedy
And the wild animal is tragic most
When man adopts death's ingenuity,
Then this was tragic. But what each had lost
Was less and more than this, which was the ghost
Of some primeval joke, now in bad taste,
Which saw no less than war, no more than waste.

4   *Not So Simple*

Haiku, says the translator, is yes and no at once,
Something and nothing, this and this-not made one.
Well, 'we are the barbarians' perhaps,
Minds trained on nothing but mind's insolence,
Vulgarians who expect
Poems – if not flowers – to be circumspect.

The single flower is more perfect than
The herbaceous border. Yet here a word can sprout
Opposites in itself, be rank and lush
As the careless garden of a careless man.
Three lines can simply mean
Something is being (will be) in the mind (or scene.)

But that is not the heart of it by half:
Language is difficult, flowers can be seen
Simply. The heart of it is everywhere
Where things are, under the nervous masking laugh,
Not permanent at all.
An earthquake, or your elbow, cracks the wall.

Too many people wanting to eat too much,
The gentle gesture is more hustled now:
Children and gardens coddled, held too tight,
Cramp your great clumsiness, brittle at a touch.
One word is 'food'; it means
Simply whether your belly has rice and beans.

Houses are also less like poems and flowers,
Though easy to destroy; one spark can be
Quite unequivocal with a city of them.
To make an Act of God uniquely yours
Live in a paper house,
Set match to paper, make an emptiness.

Haiku, says the translator, is yes and no at once,
Something and nothing, this and this–not made one.
'Bogus,' I quickly say, 'Nothing so simple,'
Envying that bogus elegance, though neither
Haiku nor I explain
The simple brutes – fire: hunger: earthquake: pain.

He escaped the ninety million
To find a lonelier place
And each day found him sitting
Admiring nature's face
In the lake where, fifty feet below,
Great carp he never saw
Could watch the casual suicide
Clutching at a straw.

At first reflecting water
Straightened the city's stance.
The headlines' daily tragedies
Drowned in that bland expanse:
A boat moored in a sandy bay
And a hill on either hand
Were kinder to his blunted eyes,
Easier to understand.

And yet the gentle pastoral
Was soured at last, for he
Found in each grain of nature
Pathetic fallacy:
The yammering cicadas,
The moths smashed on the pane
Became his symbols. And the lake
Choked with atomic rain.

These second-hand impressions,
Each image half-aware
Of some illustrious ancestor
Who looked on nature bare,
Made him no happier; but then
(He thought) 'Nothing can pass
Between the sight and seer without
Distortion in the glass.

The narrow islands fester,
Steeped in their own dung,
Yet words in this backwater are
Too easy on the tongue.
The lake's isolation
Leads me too much astray,
Smothers the suicide's gesture with
What I don't want to say.'

Back to the ninety million
He soberly returned;
Resumed vicarious misery;
Sat restlessly; then burned
Some manuscripts; and pondered
On grief and happiness
And the smooth, lonely abstractions
He could not now express.

6 *Japan: Aesthetic Point*

Flower, yellow against green:
A jot of mist between
It and the autumn tree.
Well, this is what you see
In fact, a painted screen,
Somebody's artistry.

But it is *real*, you say,
No one made it that way.
Not paint but its own pigment,
Not silk but fabric sent
Through natural roots: display
No artist ever meant.

You say these people hold
The secret, lost of old,
Which life and art should share.
These patterns do not stare
Me in the face, too bold
For here or anywhere.

Still, there is always this
Side to such mysteries —
Small boys, all about six,
Beating with stones and sticks
A butterfly which is
Beyond these aesthetics.

Being not quite dead, it stirs
Feebly. The eye prefers
Death patterned on a screen.
Its yellow and its green
Lie smashed. The artist blurs
The too deliberate scene.

So this is life and that
Is art, the duplicate
Which stares life in the face,
And this uncanny race,
So cruel, so delicate,
Shows each its separate place.

7 *To My Unborn Child*

Nothing is known but that you are
And move under her hand and mine,
Feeding and sleeping, clandestine
Agent and close conspirator.
You mould your own unique design
And grow frail roots nine months in her.

Collision of erratic spores
Moved eyes to bud, fingers to swell
Out of the light, and now he walks
On water, and is miracle.

What you will be the uncertain world
Waits for and watches, nor can make
Provision for each loose mistake
You drop when, far beyond the fold,
The days you pass, the routes you take
Teach you to be shy or bold.

The tent of flesh, the hut of bone
Shelter him on pilgrimage
And blood and water build for him
A flooded road, a shifting bridge.

Not yet real, we make for you
A toy that is reality.
The secret country where you lie
Is far from it, but no less true,
And both are dangerous to the eye
That fears what flesh and fate may do.

Tent, hut and bridge are weak as he
And yet unnumbered travellers
Have spent dark nights encamped in such
Retreats, and trod such paths as hers.

You who will soon step down through blood
To where earth, sky and air combine
To make you neither hers nor mine,
Think: you now stand where many stood
Who, each in his own unique design,
Was weak and strong and bad and good.

And yet these murmurs cannot break
The doors which you alone unbar,
And we who know all this must know
Nothing is known but that you are.

8   *Child Crying*

My daughter cries, and I
Lift her from where she lies,
Carry her here and there,
Talk nonsense endlessly.
And still she cries and cries
In rage, mindlessly.

A trivial anguish, found
In every baby-book.
But, at a fortnight old,
A pink and frantic mound
Of appetites, each look
Scans unfamiliar ground.

A name without a face
Becomes a creature, takes
A creature's energies.
Raging in my embrace,
She takes the world and shakes
Each firm appointed place.

No language blocks her way,
Oblique, loaded with tact.
Hunger and pain are real,
And in her blindness they
Are all she sees: the fact
Is what you cannot say.

Our difference is that
We gauge what each cry says,
Supply what need demands.
Or try to. All falls flat
If cure is wrong or guess
Leaves her still obdurate.

So through uncertainties
I carry her here and there,
And feel her human heart,
Her human miseries,
And in her language share
Her blind and trivial cries.

from *The Owl in the Tree*

9 Things

Some lie in a specimen-case
In a jumble of randomness,
Things I have picked up
From the ground or a junk-shop tray:
A terracotta lamp,
An ammonite, a toad
Carved from an old root,
Worked flints, a handful of sherds,
A bamboo whistle, stones
Rubbed and shaped by the sea,
And a snuff-box with a loose lid.
Others pile high on shelves
Or get stacked up on the floor:
Magazines, albums, jugs.
Walled up, I sit among things.

Elsewhere, in the attic or drawers,
Are letters, programmes, notes
On backs of envelopes, guides
To castles, postcards, stamps.
One of these days, we say,
We'll sort the whole lot out,
Tie things in bundles, throw
Most of the clobber away.
But we never shall, of course.
My pockets bulge with stuff
After walking through a ploughed field.
Things stick to me like burrs,
Or muck to a caddis worm.
Freud has explained it all
But not, somehow, to me.

Hoarding a load of crap
May be hoarding a load of crap
To the analyst; but I think
What I really want is things

To tell me what I have been.
I cosset my memory
Like some people their cat.
And that, I suppose, is a way
Of saying that I'm ashamed
To go on collecting stuff.
True: somewhere in my mind
Is an ideal picture of life
In a bare unfurnished room
With a notebook and pen. But then
What would I have to say?

10 *The Boys*

Six of them climbed aboard,
None of them twenty yet,
At a station up the line:
Flannel shirts rimmed with sweat,
Boots bulled to outrageous shine,
Box-pleats stiff as a board.

Pinkly, smelling of Bass,
They lounged on the blue moquette
And rubbed their blanco off.
One told of where to get
The best crumpet. A cough
From the corner. One wrote on the glass

A word in common use.
The others stirred and jeered.
Reveille was idled through
Till the next station appeared,
And the six of them all threw
Their Weights on the floor. Excuse

For a laugh on the platform. Then
We rattled and moved away,
The boys only just through the door.
It was near the end of the day.
Two slept. One farted and swore,
And went on about his women.

Three hours we had watched this lot,
All of us family men,
Responsible, set in our ways.
I looked at my paper again:
Another H-test. There are days
You wonder whether you're not

Out of touch, old hat, gone stale.
I remembered my twenty-first
In the NAAFI, laid out cold.
Then one of them blew and burst
A bag; and one of the old
Told them to stow it. The pale

Lights of the city came near.
We drew in and stopped. The six
Bundled their kit and ran.
'A good belting would sort out their tricks,'
Said my neighbour, a well-spoken man.
'Yes, but . . .' But he didn't hear.

11 Mr Cooper

Two nights in Manchester: nothing much to do,
One of them I spent partly in a pub,
Alone, quiet, listening to people who
Didn't know me. *So I told the bloody sub-*
Manager what he could do with it. . . . Mr Payne
Covers this district – you'll have met before?
Caught short, I looked for the necessary door
And moved towards it; could hear, outside, the rain.

The usual place, with every surface smooth
To stop, I suppose, the aspirations of
The man with pencil stub and dreams of YOUTH
AGED 17. And then I saw, above
The stall, a card, a local jeweller's card
Engraved with name, JEWELLER AND WATCHMENDER
FOR FIFTY YEARS, address, telephone number.
I heard the thin rain falling in the yard.

The card was on a sort of shelf, just close
Enough to let me read this on the front.
Not, I'd have said, the sort of words to engross
Even the keenest reader, nothing to affront
The public decency of Manchester.
And yet I turned it over. On the back
Were just three words in rather smudgy black
Soft pencil: MR COOPER – DEAD. The year

Grew weakly green outside, in blackened trees,
Wet grass by statues. It was ten to ten
In March in Manchester. Now, ill at ease
And made unsure of sense and judgement when
Three words could throw me, I walked back into
The bar, where nothing much had happened since
I'd left. A man was trying to convince
Another man that somehow someone knew

Something that someone else had somehow done.
Two women sat and drank the lagers they
Were drinking when I'd gone. If anyone
Knew I was there, or had been, or might stay,
They didn't show it. *Good night*, I almost said,
Went out to find the rain had stopped, walked back
To my hotel, and felt the night, tall, black,
Above tall roofs. And Mr Cooper dead.

12   *An Enquiry*

'Hello. Mrs Newton? You won't know me but
I'm making an enquiry, some research
Into the marital problems of our time.
My name. . . ? Dr Fell. Now I wonder if
You'd mind answering a few questions for me.
In confidence, of course.' Five floors above
The Ring Road, in a block of flats, alone
She sits and hears his decent level voice.
No terrified suspicion squats beside
The telephone she holds: for nowadays
People are asking questions everywhere
Of perfect strangers. Television-men
Brandish their little pencil-microphones
At anybody, and you have to speak.
'Now first, how long have you been married? Yes.
Number of children? Mm. Your husband's job?
There's quite a lot of detail to this work –
Enquiries need to have a mass of facts . . .'
Bored, with James up on business in Carlisle,
Nothing to watch, the children tucked in bed,
She warms a little to such confidence,
Telling the Doctor what time James gets home,
Who washes up at night, and how they spend
An average evening. 'And now, if you'll please
Answer a few more intimate questions, I . . .'

Quite suddenly, the brisk enquiring voice
Takes on the low drone of a shut-in fly
Circling the glowing magnet of the light.
'In bed . . . he tears your clothes off . . . then he
    ties . . .
Hands . . . breasts . . . puts his . . . are you listening. . . ?
Tell me what it feels like . . . every bit . . .
You let him . . . please say something . . . does he
    make. . . ?'
She holds the black and swollen instrument
Away, and lets a scream gush out of her
Which, magnified and twisted through its coils,
Reaches him, 'Dr Fell', panting, alone,
His white face staring from a call-box where
He's satisfied and spent. The line goes dead.
He pushes at the door, and feels the cold.

13 *Sunday Afternoons*

On Sunday afternoons
In winter, snow in the air,
People sit thick as birds
In the station buffet-bar.
They know one another.
Some exchange a few words
But mostly they sit and stare
At the urns and the rock buns.

Not many trains today.
Not many are waiting for trains
Or waiting for anything
Except for the time to pass.
The fug is thick on the glass
Beyond which, through honks and puffing,
An express shrugs and strains
To sidings not far away.

Here no one is saying goodbye:
Tears, promises to write,
Journeys, are not for them.
Here there are other things
To mull over, till the dark brings
Its usual burdensome
Thoughts of a place for the night,
A bit of warm and dry.

On Sunday afternoons
The loudspeaker has little to say
Of wherever the few trains go.
Not many are travellers.
But few are as still as these
Who sit here out of the snow,
Passing the time away
Till the night begins.

14 *County Hotel, Edinburgh*

'Miss Minnes spends each winter with us here:
October through to May.' In the lounge
Miss Minnes sits and knots her hair
Through two bony fingers, and seems to cringe

When anyone walks by her. 'Yes, she comes
Of a very good family, up Inverness way.'
Miss Minnes sits doing complicated sums,
Dressed in a leather jerkin, day after day.

'She never speaks to anyone.' Long white face
Where eyes lie sunk in dreams, or maybe not.
In the television parlour she takes her place
For a minute or two, and then stalks out to sit

In the lounge and knot her hair and stare, stare
At the two electric bars which warm the room
From October through to May. If people cared
For Miss Minnes's seventy years, would she assume

They only meddled? 'Money's no object there.'
Among the debris of *The Field*, *The Sphere*
And last week's *Scotsman*, she, with lank grey hair,
Sits silent, twitching, winter by wintry year.

15   *The Fly*

The fly's sick whining buzz
Appals me as I sit
Alone and quietly,
Reading and hearing it
Banging against the pane,
Bruised, falling, then again
Starting his lariat tour
Round and round my head
Ceiling to wall to floor.

But I equip myself
To send him on his way,
Newspaper clutched in hand
Vigilant, since he may
Settle, shut off his shriek
And lie there mild and weak
Who thirty seconds ago
Drove air and ears mad
With shunting to and fro.

And I shall not pretend
To any well of pity
Flowing at such a death.
The blow is quick. Maybe
The Hindu's moved to tears
But not a hundred years
Of brooding could convince
My reason that this fly
Has rights which might prevent
My choosing that he die.

And yet I know the weight
Of small deaths weighs me down,
That life (whatever that is)
Is holy: that I drown
In air which stinks of death
And that each unthought breath
Takes life from some brief life,
And every step treads under
Some fragments still alive.
The fly screams to the thunder.

Death troubles me more rarely
Than when, at seventeen,
I looked at Chatterton
And thought what it might mean.
I know my children sleep
Sound in the peace they keep.
And then, suddenly calm,
The fly rests on the wall
Where he lies still, and I
Strike once. And that is all.

Twitching the leaves just where the drainpipe clogs
In ivy leaves and mud, a purposeful
Creature about its business. Dogs
Fear his stiff seriousness. He chews away

At beetles, worms, slugs, frogs. Can kill a hen
With one snap of his jaws, can taunt a snake
To death on muscled spines. Old countrymen
Tell tales of hedgehogs sucking a cow dry.

But this one, cramped by houses, fences, walls,
Must have slept here all winter in that heap
Of compost, or have inched by intervals
Through tidy gardens to this ivy bed.

And here, dim-eyed, but ears so sensitive
A voice within the house can make him freeze,
He scuffs the edge of danger: yet can live
Happily in our nights and absences.

A country creature, wary, quiet and shrewd,
He takes the milk we give him, when we're gone.
At night, our slamming voices must seem crude
To one who sits and waits for silences.

After the darkness has come
And the distant 'planes catch fire
In the dusk, coming home,
And the tall church spire
No longer stands on the hill
And the streets are quiet except
For a car-door slamming – well,
You might say the houses slept.
An owl calls from a tree.

This is my house and home,
A place where for several years
I've settled, to which I've come
Happily, set my shears
To the hedge which fronts the place,
Had decorators in,
Altered a former face
To a shape I can call my own.
An owl calls from a tree.

Only, sometimes at night
Or running downhill for a train,
I suddenly catch sight
Of a world not named and plain
And without hedges or walls:
A jungle of noises, fears,
No lucid intervals,
No calm exteriors.
An owl calls from a tree.

The place I live in has
A name on the map, a date
For all that is or was.
I avoid hunger and hate:
I have a bed for the night:
The dishes are stacked in the rack:
I remember to switch off the light:
I turn and lie on my back.
An owl calls from a tree.

Darker than eyes shut in a darkened room,
Colder than coldest hours before the dawn,
My nightmare body leaves its bed to walk
Across the unseen lawn
Where apples nudge my feet. They force a shout
Inside my throat which, struggling, can't get out.

I am awake. The dream is over now.
No one is in the garden, nor has been.
You lie beside me while I count the things
Tomorrow will begin
In idleness, omission or false choice,
In lack of purpose or uncertain voice.

You sleep, and in the dark I hear you breathe
Through certainties, responsibilities.
Sometimes you tell me of your own strange dreams.
Mine are banalities,
Trudging down trodden paths to find a heap
Of fragments unromanticized by sleep.

Letters unwritten: papers on my desk:
Money: my age: things I would not have said
Given another minute to decide.
I stifle in my bed,
Searching for other names to call it by,
This blankness which comes down so finally.

But names are nothing, dreams are nothing, when
The day unrolls itself from second sleep.
Reluctantly, I wake: shave: choose a tie.
These daily things are cheap,
The small wage paid to keep my nightmares small:
Trivial, dull: not terrible at all.

Not much is simple: you can never say
Straight out what ten more minutes will make worse.
The clean page, the new cheque-book, never stay
Like that, like the morning far too bright to last.
Reading a poem over, you can rehearse
Till the words are no longer there. The past
Silts up, stifles, practice ruins the trick.
My mind gropes at simple arithmetic.

Gropes, and misses its footing. All the time, you're sure
That the line is straight, the page turned, the thought
At the back of your mind needs only a nudge to cure
The uncertainty. Every three months or so
I clear my desk, discovering what I ought
To have thrown away at once three months ago.
And then it's simple: except to dither over
Trash, scraps I never wanted to discover.

Not much is simple: water, sleep, the pure
Labour of digging a patch of ground. But then
You can't live on these. What makes me feel secure
The times when I am, isn't simple at all—
The ordering of time, the punctual skills, the pen
Flowing without a blot: a miracle
That out of disorder even so much can be
Simple. I jib at the word *complexity*.

And I am right, I suppose. A home, a wife,
Children, are simple properties, whose care
And love and order frame a simple life.
Valuing this is easy, keeping it
Much harder: for, come pat and unaware,
And stealthily, a bland indefinite
Ghost blots the page, clutters the desk, and says
'Not much is simple, nevertheless.'

This blackbird stared at us six feet away,
Set in a hedge, its poise at once too pure,
Too sure and still to be a real bird:
We, in the room, through glass, watched it and still
Without fear, in the hedge, it stood and watched us too.

Caught in the moment of alighting, died.

Caught by no cat: I looked for blood, or mess
Of feathers disarrayed. And certainly no hawk.
Here – where the suburbs cheat a violent death
By natural tooth or claw – it gripped a twig
With each long plucking claw, fanned out its wings,
Threw back its head and beak.
                                        Only its eyes,
Glazed to opaqueness, said that something died.

My daughter, three years old, whose practical eyes
See spiders, flies and ladybirds asleep,
Who lays out berries for them when they wake,
Asked me what I would do. 'I'll bury it –
Put it in a hole.' 'And will it hide like me?'

No need, though, for such ceremony as this.
We left the bird – memento, incident
Strange in the level course of things – all night.
In the morning, nothing. The leaves ruffled where
It took its stance, one of them crumpled by
The gripping claw. A hole where nothing was
Before or after. Buried in blank air.

This small death, vanishing from time and place,
Left this small gap, a childish question asked
And never answered: 'Why did the bird go?'
Well, common sense would answer with a cat
Prowling from neighbouring gardens. Maybe so.
And yet, dead of old age or whatever else,

Those wings, heraldic, that full throat thrust back,
Those blind white eyes, announced some hiding-place
Shared with the spider, ladybird and fly,
With child and man. And could not tell us why.

21 *At Birth*

Come from a distant country,
Bundle of flesh, of blood,
Demanding painful entry,
Expecting little good:
There is no going back
Among those thickets where
Both night and day are black
And blood's the same as air.

Strangely you come to meet us,
Stained, mottled, as if dead:
You bridge the dark hiatus
Through which your body slid
Across a span of muscle,
A breadth my hand can span.
The gorged and brimming vessel
Flows over, and is man.

Dear daughter, as I watched you
Come crumpled from the womb,
And sweating hands had fetched you
Into this world, the room
Opened before your coming
Like water struck from rocks
And echoed with your crying
Your living paradox.

After the usual rounds at night
In the house and property called my own,
Front door, back door, bolted tight;
Fire raked down; stove stoked high –
I climbed the stairs and there, alone
On the landing by the nursery,
I saw my daughter watching me.

In fact, a baby in her cot
Asleep, beyond that firm closed door.
But twenty years from now, and not
Our sole sweet charge, our special grace,
She stood like someone glimpsed before
In book or crowd: and in her face
The future marked its time and place.

I knew she was not real, and gone
Within a moment. So I went
Through all the trivial jobs, and on
To bed. But, half asleep, I lay
And wondered how impermanent
The future is, yet day by day
My daughter walks it on its way.

That daughter will not be my own
As house and property are mine,
For in that moment I was shown
A stranger at my baby's door,
A stranger made by some design
Not ours, and hammered out before
She took the shape her mother bore.

But in a curious happiness
I faced that fact, and knew at once
That child and woman would express
Through every known and unknown thing

(Each of them her inheritance)
A permanence in everything,
While acquisitions clog and cling.

She sleeps so light that if I go
Into her room, she turns and stirs.
The house is quiet, its rooms all show
A locked and barred security.
And in my sleep, deeper than hers,
I watch her stand and look at me,
Stripped of possessions and made free.

23   *Looking On*

Hearing our voices raised –
Perhaps in anger,
Or in some trivial argument
That is not anger –
She screams until we stop,
And smile, and look at her,
Poised on the sheer drop
Which opens under her.

If these, her parents, show
How the gods can fail,
Squabbling on Olympus,
How can she fail
To see that anarchy
Is what one must expect,
That to be happy
One must be circumspect?

But the reverse is true
Also, when we kiss,
Seeing herself excluded
Even from that kiss.

The gods' too gross affairs
Made myths for innocent men,
So the innocent eye stares
At love in its den.

Like a strange motley beast
Out of an old myth,
Anger and love together
Make up her own myth
Of these two who cherish,
Protect, feed, deny,
In whose arms she will flourish
Or else will die.

24   *Sick Child*

Lit by the small night-light you lie
And look through swollen eyes at me:
Vulnerable, sleepless, try
To stare through a blank misery,
And now that boisterous creature I
Have known so often shrinks to this
Wan ghost unsweetened by a kiss.

Shaken with retching, bewildered by
The virus curdling milk and food,
You do not scream in fear, or cry.
Tears are another thing, a mood
Given an image, infancy
Making permitted show of force,
Boredom, or sudden pain. The source

Of this still vacancy's elsewhere.
Like my sick dog, ten years ago,
Who skulked away to some far lair
With poison in her blood: you know

Her gentleness, her clouded stare,
Pluck blankets as she scratched the ground.
She made, and you now make, no sound.

The rank smell shrouds you like a sheet.
Tomorrow we must let crisp air
Blow through the room and make it sweet,
Making all new. I touch your hair,
Damp where the forehead sweats, and meet—
Here by the door, as I leave you—
A cold, quiet wind, chilling me through.

25 *White Snow*

'White snow,' my daughter says, and sees
For the first time the lawn, the trees,
Loaded with this superfluous stuff.
Two words suffice to make facts sure
To her, whose mental furniture
Needs only words to say enough.

Perhaps by next year she'll forget
What she today saw delicate
On every blade of grass and stone;
Yet will she recognize those two
Syllables, and see them through
Eyes which remain when snow has gone?

Season by season, she will learn
The names when seeds sprout, leaves turn,
And every change is commonplace.
She will bear snowfalls in the mind,
Know wretchedness of rain and wind,
With the same eyes in a different face.

My wish for her, who held by me
Looks out now on this mystery
Which she has solved with words of mine,
Is that she may learn to know
That in her words for the white snow
Change and permanence combine—
The snow melted, the trees green,
Sure words for hurts not suffered yet, nor seen.

26   *House for Sale*

A house gone derelict where, splayed
Like metal branches, pipes jut out
Where once the Ascot hung: we tread,
Disturbing letters on the mat
Pushed through the door a year ago—
'The Owner, No. 6'—and blow
Dust from the mantelpiece. The soot
Slops in the grate and, underfoot,
Goes tracking everywhere we go.

Each twelve by ten of empty room
Marks out a musty cell, which bed,
Chair, table, hideous jug made seem
A kind of home inherited
By someone we have never known.
Yet nothing by itself has grown
To make it permanent, and now
Patches of wall alone show how
A man had made it look his own.

Tramping through vacant echoes, we
Sniff out the damp and scuff at floors,
Knock plaster from the ceiling, see
Mouseholes in cellars, wrench at doors
That will not open. Windows face
Into the yard where weeds embrace
The neighbourhood's old wheels and tins,
A sluggish commerce which begins
To mould it to a different place.

Living in this, could we begin
To set to rights what others left
In casual indiscipline,
Its grace or ugliness bereft?
Houses, indeed, are flimsy stuff,
For mortar is not strong enough
To keep an emptiness alive,
And chairs and tables can't revive
The rooms which they were tenants of.

Where people live – known rooms, or those
Windows through which we look and see
Families round tables, doors that close
On lived-in places – these are free
Of everything we pry through here:
The blank foundations where we peer
On unknown lives which, moving on,
Have told us only that they've gone
And what they've left we cannot share.

How, after thirty years of not
Much daring wildness or bad luck,
Do I have so many? No one shot
At me from rooftops, ran me down,
Used me for bayonet practice. Stuck
In small remembered moments, they
Mark even smaller wounds: yet have grown
As I have, to this very day.

The palm of my right hand, scraped raw
By ash and gravel, takes me to
Myself at seventeen: I saw
The athlete had some praise I lacked,
And so I ran for the House. I grew
Hearty and keen. And then one day
I slipped at relay-practice, cracked
My wrist and tore the flesh away.

A bit of travel, too: one thigh
Grazed by stony reefs at sea
Off Libya, swimming: and by
My left wrist, where a window fell
At thirteen in Vermont, I see
A quarter of an inch of white.
A doctor's room in Muswell Hill
Made one of them. A certain light

Shows up one eyebrow ruffled where
A beer glass hit it, up in Leeds –
My only brawl. The bristly hair
At the tip of my chin is sparse because
At nine I fell off a chair. It bleeds
Still, if I close my eyes. Yet not
One rates my passport; minor flaws,
So minor that they show me what

A whole half lifetime did not wound.
There is just one I can't explain:
A thin curved band which goes half round
My little finger, like a ring.
It must have hurt, and yet the pain
Means nothing to me: like the scars
I've never worn, like suffering
Not named in small particulars.

28 *At Enoshima*

Level and grey, the sea moves from the east
Carrying fish-heads, cartons, broken glass:
Here a rice barrel bursts out of its staves,
Chicken-bones crunch under as I pass.
The holy island does without a priest
But catches tourists after souvenirs,
So picnic litter sprawls in with the waves
To leave a scurf along this stretch of sand,
Cast-offs and shiftings of the shifting land.

And it is here, along that wavering path
Of plastic lemonade jars, bottles, straws,
I find this other souvenir of Japan,
Swept in by tides to join the common shore's
Museum of rejection: a thin lath,
A pointed stake, a spar of wood, a grave
Not made of lasting stuff, to mark a man
Whose name I cannot read, an age and date
I puzzle out like an illiterate.

He died two months ago, in March. It's just
Those characters I know. The flowing brush
Moves elegantly on, leaves me behind
To dumbly feel the holy island crush
That body, now anonymous, to dust.

Whatever else he was I do not know,
Except his dying left for me to find
His cheap memorial. Ignorant, foreign, I
See nothing but this wood, this mystery.

29   The Barrow

In this high field strewn with stones
I walk by a green mound,
Its edges sheared by the plough.
Crumbs of animal bone
Lie smashed and scattered round
Under the clover leaves
And slivers of flint seem to grow
Like white leaves among green.
In the wind, the chestnut heaves
Where a man's grave has been.

Whatever the barrow held
Once, has been taken away:
A hollow of nettles and dock
Lies at the centre, filled
With rain from a sky so grey
It reflects nothing at all.
I poke in the crumbled rock
For something they left behind
But after that funeral
There is nothing at all to find.

On the map in front of me
The gothic letters pick out
Dozens of tombs like this,
Breached, plundered, left empty,
No fragments littered about
Of a dead and buried race
In the margins of histories.

No fragments: these splintered bones
Construct no human face,
These stones are simply stones.

In museums their urns lie
Behind glass, and their shaped flints
Are labelled like butterflies.
All that they did was die,
And all that has happened since
Means nothing to this place.
Above long clouds, the skies
Turn to a brilliant red
And show in the water's face
One living, and not these dead.

30 *Manhood End*

At Manhood End the older dead lie thick
Together by the churchyard's eastern wall.
The sexton sweated out with spade and pick
And moved turf, clay, bones, gravestones, to make room
For later comers, those whose burial
Was still far off, but who would need a tomb.

Among the pebbles, in the molehills' loam,
Turned thighbone up, and skull: whatever frail
Relic was left was given a new home,
Close to the wood and farther from the sea.
Couch-grass grew stronger here and, with the pale
Toadstools and puffballs, masked that vacancy.

In April, on a day when rain and sun
Had stripped all distances to clarity,
I stood there by the chapel, and saw one
Lean heron rising on enormous wings
Across the silted harbour towards the sea.
Dead flowers at my feet: but no one brings

Flowers to those shifted bodies. The thin flies,
First flies of spring, stirred by the rain-butt. Names
Stared at me out of moss, the legacies
Of parents to their children: *Lucy, Ann,*
Names I have given, which a father claims
Because they mean something that he began.

Cool in the chapel of St. Wilfred, I
Knelt by the Saxon wall and bowed my head,
Shutting my eyes: till, looking up to high
Above the pews, I saw a monument,
A sixteenth-century carving, with the dead
Husband and wife kneeling together, meant

For piety and remembrance. But on their right
I grasped with sudden shock a scene less pure —
A naked woman, arms bound back and tight,
And breasts thrust forward to be gnawed by great
Pincers two men held out. I left, unsure
Of what that emblem meant; and towards the gate

The small mounds of the overcrowded dead
Shrank in the sun. The eastern wall seemed built
Of darker stone. I lay: and by my head
A starling with its neck snapped; nestling there,
A thrush's egg with yolk and white half spilt,
And one chafed bone a molehill had laid bare.

Frail pictures of the world at Manhood End —
How we are shifted, smashed, how stones display
The names and passions that we cannot mend.
The lych-gate stood and showed me, and I felt
The pebbles teach my feet. I walked away,
My head full of the smell my nostrils smelt.

from *The Stones of Emptiness*

I

Emptying the teapot out
Into the drain, I catch sight
Suddenly of flies at work
On some rubbish by the back
Of the shed, and standing there
Smell the small corruption where
A fishbone makes its measured path
Into the leaves, into the earth.

II

Under the raspberry canes I prod to light
Two Roman sherds, a glint of Roman glass,
A bit of bellarmine, some stoneware scraps,
And searching on might find the rougher wares,
Friable, gritty, Saxon: porous stuff
That lets the rain leak through, the dew absorb,
Frost craze and crack. *Frango*, I break, becomes
Fragment, the broken pieces to be joined
To give a date to everything we own.

III

The little duchess, aged four hundred, stirs
To feel the instruments break through the lead.
Troy stands on the nine layers of its filth
And I tread out another cigarette.

IV

Compost of feasts and leavings, thick
Layer after layer of scourings, peelings, rinds,
Bone pressed on potsherd, fish-head sieved to dust,

And in the spoil-heaps goes the fly, the quick
Mouse with her pink brood, and the maggot, slow
To render down the fat. Trash, husk, and rust,
Grass sickled, scythed, and mown, hedge-clippings, leaves,
Wet infiltrations, skins and rags of skins,
Humus of twigs and insects, skeletons
Of petals.
             Stale loaves and fishes so divided out
They feed five thousand trees, five million roots.

V

Pipes void it to the sea,
The Thames chokes on its way.
We live on what we spend,
Are spent, are lived upon.
Nothing has an end.
The compost is my son,
My daughter breeds the dust,
We become ash, air,
Water, earth, the past
Our daughters' sons share.

32 *At Dunwich*

Fifteen churches lie here
Under the North Sea;
Forty-five years ago
The last went down the cliff.
You can see, at low tide,
A mound of masonry
Chewed like a damp bun.

In the village now (if you call
Dunwich a village now,
With a handful of houses, one street,
And a shack for Tizer and tea)
You can ask an old man
To show you the stuff they've found
On the beach when there's been a storm:

Knife-blades, buckles and rings,
Enough coins to fill an old sock,
Badges that men wore
When they'd been on pilgrimage,
Armfuls of broken pots.
People cut bread, paid cash,
Buttoned up against the cold.

Fifteen churches, and men
In thousands working at looms,
And wives brewing up stews
In great grey cooking pots.
I put out a hand and pull
A sherd from the cliff's jaws.
The sand trickles, then falls.

Nettles grow on the cliffs
In clumps as high as a house.
The houses have gone away.
Stand and look at the sea
Eating the land as it walks
Steadily treading the tops
Of fifteen churches' spires.

33 *Underneath*

From someone's transistor a quarter-mile away
The sound of someone's band lifts over gardens
And finds me here examining a weed
Trowelled up among hundreds in the patch of waste
At the end of this narrow bit of property
I own on the edge of London, where the clay
Starts one spade down, going as far below
As the roof of my house is high, and reaching water
Clear underneath, held in its caves and pockets,
Trapped, unevaporating, silent, cold,
But working back through roots and tall foundations
To mushroom up anywhere, now here
In the roots of the three-leafed weed I hold in my hand,
Disturbed for a moment by that distant band.

34 *The Pond*

With nets and kitchen sieves they raid the pond,
Chasing the minnows into bursts of mud,
Scooping and chopping, raking up frond after frond
Of swollen weed after a week of flood.

Thirty or forty minnows bob and flash
In every jam-jar hoarded on the edge,
While the shrill children with each ill-aimed splash
Haul out another dozen as they dredge.

Choked to its banks, the pond spills out its store
Of frantic life. Nothing can drain it dry
Of what it breeds: it breeds so effortlessly
Theft seems to leave it richer than before.

The nostrils snuff its rank bouquet – how warm,
How lavish, foul, and indiscriminate, fat
With insolent appetite and thirst, so that
The stomach almost heaves to see it swarm.

But trapped in glass the minnows flail and fall,
Sink, with upended bellies showing white.
After an hour I look and see that all
But four or five have died. The greenish light

Ripples to stillness, while the children bend
To spoon the corpses out, matter-of-fact,
Absorbed: as if creation's prodigal act
Shrank to this empty jam-jar in the end.

35 *Lesson*

In the big stockyards, where pigs, cows, and sheep
Stumble towards the steady punch that beats
All sense out of a body with one blow,
Certain old beasts are trained to lead the rest
And where they go the young ones meekly go.

Week after week these veterans show the way,
Then, turned back just in time, are led themselves
Back to the pens where their initiates wait.
The young must cram all knowledge in one day,
But the old who lead live on and educate.

Solemn administrator, cowled creature
Ruling your lines in a book devised for
Recording our customs and our nature,

You impel such movements as keep us alive,
Eating, sleeping, always on the move
To the place where we must never arrive –

For that would be to break your rhythm,
Allowing us too easily to become
Mere animals of irregular stab and spasm.

Yet you are animal too: all of us know
That Pavlov's dog salivated for you,
That you tell the log-rolling elephant what he must do.

Patron of babies and the very old,
Adversary of clerks dreaming of Gauguin, shield
Of sergeant-majors doing what they are told;

Keep you as we may, singly or bunched together,
You grow into one hard carapace whatever
Soft twigs and shoots underneath wanly stir.

Put in compartments, like a honeycomb
You spill from cell to cell, leaving no room,
Stifling with sweet indulgence all who come

Prying or bustling, scouring with mop and rake.
On holiday, you are the last thing we take
But take you we do, and when it's over bring you back.

If we break you, we may get fat, grow young, go mad,
Wondering why we listened to what you said
Or wondering in the end whether you're all we've had.

Resented, you weigh us down like Atlas his world:
Cherished, you allow us without pain to grow old:
When we die, our children inherit you before we are cold.

37 Two Faces

One gets inured to having the wrong face.
For years I thought it soft, too pink and young
To match that shrewd, mature, and self-possessed
Person behind it. In a forced grimace
I saw all that I *should* have been, the strong
Line linking nose to mouth, the net of care
Fixed by the concentration of the eyes.
Such marks upon the lineaments expressed
Things that I wanted most, but would not dare,
Prevented by the innocence I despised.

Yet now, this morning, as I change a blade,
Look up and clear the glass, I recognize
Some parody of that scored, experienced man.
But this one, as I take it, seems afraid
Of what he sees, is hesitant, with his eyes
Shifting away from something at my back.
No, this is not the one I recognized
Proleptically in mirrors; neither can
He any longer see what firm lines track
Back to that innocence he once despised.

Two ram's horns married with a bit of gut
Wail on the pavement near the Sport Café
As Mustafa and I walk by the shut
Emporia this blue December Friday.

Mustafa wears a trim Italian suit,
Reads Sartre in the Faculty of Arts,
Writes poems behind dark glasses, is acute
About 'some' and 'any' and the various parts

Of speech. He will go far – maybe in Oil.
Whereas this flautist, swathed in motley shawls,
Unshaved, one-eyed, from whom the dogs recoil,
Seems at a dead end. Poverty appals

More when it sweetly insinuates and smiles.
Mustafa notices. 'A marabout,' he says,
Explaining the presence: explanation reconciles.
I notice the moth-holes in the faded fez.

'That man is wise and holy,' Mustafa says,
And puts a piastre in the wizened hand.
I avoid his glance. To Allah let there be praise.
Round Barclay's DCO the armed guards stand.

Isaiah 34: 11

Eroded slabs, collapsed and weathered tables,
Porous and pocked limestone, rubble of schist:
They are the real blocks where the real foot stumbles,
Boulders where lizards move like Medusa's prey
Freed from their stone trance. Here the stone-eyed exist
Among pebbles, fossil-bearing images
Glaring their life-in-death in the blinding day.
At the dark cave's mouth they stand like effigies.

They define the void. They assert
How vast the distances are, featureless, bare.
Their absence creates the extremest kind of desert,
A sea of sand. They are to the desolate earth
What a single hawk is to the desolate air.
And suddenly here, grouped in a circle
In the middle of nowhere, they form a hearth
Round a fire long since dead, built by an unknown people.

The soil profitless under their strewn acres,
Even so they harbour in their ungenerous shade
Flowers as delicate as they themselves are fierce.
Scorpions entrench under them, flat as dry leaves.
In parched wadi beds, coagulate in a blockade
Against all but a man on foot, who, waterless
And far from home, stumbles as he perceives
Only that line of confusion, the stones of emptiness.

Beautiful only when the light catches it
Arrested yet volatile in a shaft of sun,
Or under the microscope, like an ancient detritus
Of snowflakes: otherwise valueless debris.
The ash from my cigarette, the air from my lungs,
The soles of my shoes, the palms of my hands, breed it,
Absorb it, carry it, disperse it. The liquids of bodies
Dry to it in the end, and the sea's salt.

Created from the beginning, it carries its beginnings
Even to the end. Metals and minerals
Are crushed to its substance: in the desert
It is beyond the harshness of sand. Soft,
Disposable, it collects in corners, to be moved
Only to another place: it cannot be moved
Finally. Indestructible, even in fire
It shapes its own phoenix, and rises with the wind.

Each second shifts it, animates its grey
Weight, bearing down on pliant surfaces.
Analyse its origins, and you find the full range
Of everything living and dead. It obeys water,
Lying down to a drenching, but as the sun
Parches that adversary it re-forms and spreads
Further and further, to the eyes, the nostrils, the throat,
A thin dry rain, contemptible, persistent.

In a world of definable objects, each different from each,
It unites as denominator of all,
The common agent. I see the white page
Gathering its random calligraphy under my pen,
And see at the tip of the pen the fine motes swirl
Down to that point where a fragmented earth
Silently whirls in an air choked with nothing but dust:
The pulverization of planets, the universe dust.

The green encrusted lump
Stews in its vinegar.
I peck with a pocket knife
At accretions of shell and stone.
Sand flakes from the centre.

After three days of this
The alchemy takes over.
Through a mask of verdigris
A profile stares through,
Wild-haired and chapleted.

And there on the other side
A vestigial horse capers
Across an illegible
Inscription in Greek. I rinse
The tiny disc at the tap.

I keep it now on my desk
With the other beachcombings,
This rendering down of the last
Twenty-five centuries
To a scoured chip of bleached bronze.

42 Buzzards Above Cyrene

Alone or in wheeling squadrons of dozens, they move
High above the escarpment, drift to the plain below,
The sun with a certain light obscuring their wings
So that they vanish to narrowed points of darkness
Only to swing away a moment later
Becoming spread sails, gold, brown, distinct and huge
Over tombs, junipers, red stones, red dust
Caught in a still and windless stretch of blue.
But more than that, they impose a scale by which
You measure these golden ruins, these hanging gardens of
    fossils,
These clear imperial edicts and pieties
Cluttering the ledges with magnificence,
All narrowed to points of light in an unwinking eye
For which, fathoms down, a mouse freezes still, a lizard
Flashes, a dung beetle labours through dry thorns,
Regarded, moved over like a dowser's twig,
To twitch then, jerk down, pounce, finding nothing there
But these poor small spoils, these puny snacks and beakfuls
Littered among ruins, squalid among remains,
Ravaged, scavenged, picked clean among pink blooms.

43 Arabic Script

Like a spider through ink, someone says, mocking: see it
Blurred on the news-sheets or in neon lights
And it suggests an infinitely plastic, feminine
Syllabary, all the diacritical dots and dashes
Swimming together like a shoal of minnows,
Purposive yet wayward, a wavering measure
Danced over meaning, obscuring vowels and breath.
But at Sidi Kreibish, among the tombs,
Where skulls lodge in the cactus roots,

The pink claws breaking headstone, cornerstone,
Each fleshy tip thrusting to reach the light,
Each spine a hispid needle, you see the stern
Edge of the language, Kufic, like a scimitar
Curved in a lash, a flash of consonants
Such as swung out of Medina that day
On the long flog west, across ruins and flaccid colonials,
A swirl of black flags, white crescents, a language of swords.

44 *Silphium*

Thick-rooted and thick-stemmed,
Its tail embracing its stem,
Its flower-globes gathered in knots,
Now dead as the dodo,
The mastodon and the quagga,
Commemorated on coins
And in hideous Fascist fountains,
It stands as panacea
For whatever ill you choose,
Since no one living has seen it
Cure dropsy, warts, or gripe,
Flavoured a stew with it,
Or slipped it with a wink
As aphrodisiacal bait.
But there it all is in the books,
Theophrastus, Strabo, Pliny,
Fetching its weight in silver
In the market at Cyrene,
Kept in the state treasury,
Sold to equip the army
By Caesar, sent to Nero
As a rare imperial prize.
Where has it gone? The carious
Teeth of the camel, perhaps,
Have munched it away, or the goat
Scouring the dry pastures.

But I cannot credit the tough
Uncomplicated grasp
Of a plant loosening hold on life
Completely: I imagine a small
Hidden cleft in the worn rock,
Shaded by prickly pear,
Nervously footed by gecko,
Where, thick-rooted and thick-stemmed,
Its tail embracing its stem,
Those flower-globes gather in knots,
That solitary stance
Eluding the oil-prospectors,
The antiquaries, the shepherds,
Who are searching for something else
And need no panacea.

45 *Ali Ben Shufti*

You want coins? Roman? Greek? Nice vase? Head of god,
    goddess?
Look, shufti here, very cheap. Two piastres? You joke.

I poke among fallen stones, molehills, the spoil
Left by the archaeologists and carelessly sieved.
I am not above ferreting out a small piece
From the foreman's basket when his back is turned.
One or two of my choicer things were acquired
During what the museum labels call 'the disturbances
Of 1941'; you may call it loot,
But I keep no records of who my vendors were –
Goatherds, Johnnies in berets, Neapolitan conscripts
Hot foot out of trouble, dropping a keepsake or two.
I know a good thing, I keep a quiet ear open when
The college bodysnatchers arrive from Chicago,
Florence, Oxford, discussing periods
And measuring everything. I've even done business with them:

You will find my anonymous presence in the excavation reports
When you get to 'Finds Locally Purchased'. Without a B.A. –
And unable to read or write – I can date and price
Any of this rubbish. Here, from my droll pantaloons
That sag in the seat, amusing you no end,
I fetch out Tanagra heads, blue Roman beads,
A Greek lamp, bronze from Byzantium,
A silver stater faced with the head of Zeus.
I know three dozen words of English, enough French
To settle a purchase, and enough Italian
To convince the austere *dottore* he's made a bargain.
As for the past, it means nothing to me but this:
A time when things were made to keep me alive.
You are the ones who go on about it: I survive
By scratching it out with my fingers. I make you laugh
By being obsequious, roguish, battered, in fact
What you like to think of as a typical Arab.
Well, Amr Ibn el-As passed this way
Some thirteen hundred years ago, and we stayed.
I pick over what he didn't smash, and you
Pay for the leavings. That is enough for me.
You take them away and put them on your shelves
And for fifty piastres I give you a past to belong to.

46 *Butterflies in the Desert*

Thrown together like leaves, but in a land
Where no leaves fall and trees wither to scrub,
Raised like the dust but fleshed as no dust is,
They impale themselves like martyrs on the glass,
Leaving their yellow stigmata. A hundred miles
And they form a screen between us and the sparse world.
At the end of the journey we see the juggernaut
Triumphant under their flattened wings, crushed fluids.
Innocent power destroys innocent power.
But who wins, when their bloody acid eats through chrome?
In the competition for martyrs, Donatus won,
But the stout churches of his heresy now stand
Ruined, emptied of virtue, choked with innocent sand.

47 *At Asqefar*

At Asqefar the German helmet
Rests like a scarecrow's bonnet
On a bare branch.
The shreds of coarse grey duffel
Hang round the gap a rifle
Left in a shallow trench.

'Much blood,' said the shepherd,
Gesturing with his head
Towards the bald hillside.
A spent cartridge nestles
Among the dry thistles.
Blood long since dried.

Strange and remote, almost,
As these old figures traced
In Asqefar's cave:
There, pictured in red clay,
Odysseus comes back from Troy
Near the German's grave.

Twenty-five years since the battle
Plucked up the sand and let it settle
On the German soldier.
Far away now the living, the dead,
Disarmed, unhelmeted,
At Troy, at Asqefar.

48 *Qasīda on the Track to Msus*

Towards sundown we came out of the valley
Along that track
Not knowing then where it led to, when we saw
The stone circles, the heaped cairns of stone, the stones
Arranged like coracles on the dry slopes.
The brown hills were empty. Only a buzzard
Stood in the sky, perceiving its territory.

Stopping, we knew the place for an encampment
Or what remained of one: the litter of pots,
The broken shafts of ploughs, battered tin bowls,
Sickles and shears rusting, the chattels of the living.
But there were the dead too, in those stone enclosures
Laid into sand below tattered banners, marked with a stone
At head and foot. For them the tents had moved on,
The blanketed camels, the donkeys heaped high
With panniers and vessels for water. And for us too:
We had passed beyond the wells and the fresh springs
Where the goats shuffled in black congregations,
Beyond even the last dry Roman cistern before Msus
At the end of a track we never intended to take.

Behind us, the barking of dogs and the wind from the sea,
Neither concerned with us nor the way south:
In front, the steppes of gazelles and scorpions
To be hunted or burned, for those who might venture
Further into that camouflage.

But, because it was sundown, we slept there and lay
Hearing the wind, watching the rising moon
Above stars falling like snow through constellations
We could not name. At dawn, we turned back
Into the accustomed valley, a settled place,
Going between tents and herds, yelped at by dogs,
Watched by threshers and gleaners, moving among men.
And still on that hillside the ragged flags fret
Over the abandoned implements and stones,
And now I shall never reach Msus,
Having turned back to the easy valley, while those
Who were not left behind rode, I suppose, south
To some name on the map I might just recognize
Or a day's ride beyond to a name I do not know.

The Letters of Synesius

Synesius of Cyrene: born in Libya *c.* A.D. 370, died there *c.* A.D. 413. Greek by ancestry, Roman by citizenship, he considered himself to be a Libyan, a citizen of the Libyan Pentapolis, of which Cyrene, his birthplace, was one city, and Ptolemais, of which he became bishop, was another. He studied under Hypatia at Alexandria, visited Athens, went as ambassador of the Pentapolis to Constantinople, and probably died at the hands of a native Libyan tribe, the Austuriani.

It seemed to me that I was some other person, and that I was one listening to myself amongst others who were present . . .

SYNESIUS to HYPATIA

*You must know my way of speaking the truth bluntly has
followed me even to the bounds of Libya.*

                                          At Tocra
The ephebes set hammer and chisel to the wall
Each in his different way, with different skills.
Well–oiled conscripts, glistening and drunk,
Inscribe their achievements and their names and die.
The dragon inherits the Hesperidean gardens
And spawns small lizards, quicksilver on white rock.
Lethe has lights. The dark pools breed white fish
Nevertheless, and blind white crayfish.
                                    Ask for the key
At the Military Academy where the Dean has just finished
Lecturing on the psychology of war.
The Jews have sacked Cyrene. In the tombs
Families sit round brewing tea.
                              Necropolis.
The Parliament building is locked. The wells are locked –
At Gasr Lebia, where Justinian's queen
Is celebrated in mosaic: bull,
Fish, amphibious monster with a conch,
An eagle preying on a calf, crab's claws,
And perched on a curiously humped crocodile
A duck.
            The wells are dry, the drillers cry for oil
And find dry holes. Concession 65
Spouts oil and blood. Great wonders come to pass.
                                    The linguists say
The Berber cannot write but has an alphabet
No one can read. Tenders are asked
For a new road to Chad.
                        Somewhere between
Brega and Zelten, in a waste of sand,
A signpost on an oil–drum indicates
GIALO across the trackless distances.

The king is old. Undergraduates
Are taught philosophy by Egyptians now.
And at Tocra a boy indicates with gestures
How wide is Gamal Nasser's world. That face
Looks down as often as the king's, and smiles
Where the old man's is fatherly but stern.

Aristippus emigrated. There was visa trouble.
A cloud of dust in the east presages war
And the coming of the goat. Pink and yellow,
The posters proclaim in fancy Gothic script
'No word pease whill illeagal Isreil exists'
And 'Palesting was not Belfor's land to promise'
(Belfor the idolatrous, Baal the Ingilizi hound).

                The ephebes have trouble
In mastering the Christian calendar,
The Latin alphabet. Teach us, they cry,
And go on strike. For the Franks, the wine is cheap
But when you walk the beach at the city's edge
The smashed Heineken bottles shine like grass:
Expensive mosaic. The earliest city lies here
Under this pile of donkeys' hooves. Dig here.
You find loom-weights from looms whose cloth has meshed
Into the sand, the salt, the lips of fossils.

I write between spells of guard between the watchtowers,
Or lecture on the English question-tag.

We have planted our fields for the fires lit by our enemies.

We have had wise men. Where are they now? we ask.
Aristippus, who taught that pleasure was highest good,
Callimachus, writing verses in his catalogue,
And, without false modesty, myself—
Synesius, mounting guard in my bishop's cope
And watching the setting sun run creases down
The great swathe of the Jebel.
                       I have seen
The Italian farmhouses house sheep and straw,
And vv il Duce flake from the pink walls,
Catching the last rays of the crumbling sun.
The fourth shore's harbours clog and choke with sand.

Severus the African, speaking slow Latin
With a Berberish accent, went on campaign.
Brute tribes were pacified, our cities flourished,
But the taxes rose, the coinage was debased
So that small coins are like water in the hand.
Our emperor died on the northern frontier
And so, in time, we turn to the east.
                     What stays
Is here, where some potter from Byzantium
Has pressed on the pot's foot his full-fleshed thumb.

The language with the unpronounceable sound
Made somewhere below the glottis inherits our tongue.
'Poets are followed by none save erring men,'
Said the Prophet, echoing Plato into the cave.

The ghaffir in his blanket under the stairs
Who prays five times a day to Allah the Good
Collects our garbage, has trachoma in one eye,
And shall assuredly inherit the Kingdom.

I would rather live a stranger among strangers.

The slopes below the cave are thick with flints.
Here they kept ammunition in the war,
And now tether a bullock to a post
Under the eaves of rock.
                                    Places of the mind only,
Unvisited oases, tracks marked
On unreliable maps by engineers
Who saw the landscape from two thousand feet.

So it might be a god would wander
Over the landscape deserted by his people,
Looking for evidence that once they loved him.
Now they are gone. Delicate microliths
Like snowflakes litter the dry slopes, among thorns.

I am writing to you to talk about emptiness
Because this is empty country, 'where ruins flourish'.

At first you are frightened of dogs, their distant barks
Coming closer across the strewn, ungrateful rock,
And perhaps you pick up stones to shy them away.
You are right, you trespass. Take tea with them, learn the words
For 'please' and 'thank you', bark in Arabic,
Or whatever language is current at the time:
Try Berber, Greek, Latin, Turkish, Italian,
Compounds of these, gibbering dialects –
You will still sweat with fear, ducking down for stones
Which, it may be, are tools fashioned by men
Without a language.
                              To call a man a dog
Is an insult in many languages, but not to dogs.
They sniff the high octane at Benina as the planes take off,
Watching the passengers who have an hour
Between London and Nairobi, the pale transients.

Their yellow fur bristles, they yawn and snap.
At Hagfet er Rejma they patrol the tents,
Watching me glean the slopes for polished flakes.
My pockets are full, my hands are empty.
Look, dogs, how empty. This landscape is yours, not mine.

52 LETTER IV

> *Such are our celebrations, seasonable and of old tradition,*
> *the good things of the poor.*

Simon of Cyrene carried the cross. No Libyan
In collar and tie will carry anything.
'A proud people,' says the handout wearily,
Explaining nothing.
                Lake Tritonis, place
Of Pallas Athene's birth, dries to a salt-pan
Where tin huts void their sewage. Erytheia,
Arethusa, Aegle, Hestia, are ghaffirs:
Their sweet songs are transistorized, relayed
From Radio Cairo across miles of sand.

A donkey and a microbus collide.
The donkey limps off, noisily urinates
By the side of the road, while the bus, crumpled like paper,
Waits for repairs and insurance policies.
The old survives by demanding nothing: the new
Frets in its expectations.
                I am supposed
To lead my flock through darkness until such time
As the Kingdom descends, there is no more call for martyrs,
And the meek inherit the earth. In the new order
My people go hungry thus to cleanse themselves.

In the month of Ramadan the rain begins
This year. It is December, and the stars
Wane above grey clouds, are obscured by them.
The sea is coldly feverish. Lightning streaks

The yellow stucco and the shuttered rooms.
The honey-casks, the oil-jars and the wine
Lie at the wharf. No one puts out to sea.

What can cure the soul? What food nourish it?
Fasting by day, they feast by night and cram
Sin down their gullets. In the church beyond the wall
The heretics draw lots for martyrdom.
I have nothing more to say of the good life,
Except – having seen so much – that to suppose
Things better rather than different is a way
Of dying only, swivelled to the past.
It is easy for me to act the Jeremiah,
To juxtapose the anomalous, debased present
With the golden fragments of a golden age.
The indigenous survives: the donkey limps off unhurt.
The silphium plants wilt in the private gardens
Since men no more expect a panacea.

Those who are to come will call our Lord a prophet
Mistaken among prophets. Spiritual pride
Gives way to pride of status, money, dress.
Unearth a marble goddess and you find
Her groin defiled with soldiers' filthiness.
The Temple of Zeus is smashed, the figurines
Pulped into lime. Farzúgha's church protects
A tribe of bats and owls. At Tansollúk
The arch is crammed with masonry and sand.

In the garrison chapel we sing 'God Save the Queen':
A proud people, enjoined to pray each week
For her and Johnson too.
                              Out of the sand
A scorpion heaves its fiery shoulders, smashed
By the spade, heavy with fire and venom. The old
Survives by demanding nothing: the new
Frets in its expectations. Simon bowed
Under the weight, the jeers. Something survives
As Ramadan and Christmas coincide
And we have little left to share but pride.

64

And who shall collect fruit from the desert?

The sea licks the shore with sly assurance
Where freestone masonry tumbles in pools.
Salt will never be worm-eaten, says the proverb:
It is the eater and preserver, fixed
Like mould on the surfaces of sherds, the fabric
Coins wrap themselves in, a sharp-tongued mineral,
The taste of thirst, the desert's brother, the sea's self.

I wait for something. The facile have a saying:
If life is hard on you, dwell in cities.
Watching the sea is a lifetime's occupation,
Empty of incident: looking inland
I see not emptiness but desolation.
The cities are fallen, Barca is forked with fire,
Ashes drift down on Tocra, Cyrene lies open
Like an enormous cave laid out for looting.
Here on the other side we have the sea
Rubbing and prying and investigating,
A faceless element, unharvested.

Cretans fish sponges: red mullet fills our plates
But we do not catch them. Red earth holds spilth of seeds
But we grow little, garner less. We have a mineral
More powerful than salt, liquid as sea,
Deep in its cave for looting, to sustain us.
Why should our old men sow, our young men reap?
The tall earth-delvers feed us royalties,
Our government takes tithes. Consider Esso:
It sows not, neither does it reap. Yet was ever
Woman arrayed like this one, in the Modern
Grocery Store, trousered, in high heels? In the desert
Her man plucks golden fruit, Hesperidean
Apples whose juice flows richly to the sea
To be drunk by silver tankers.

                              Undergraduates, you
Who sit your final examinations, consider
Omar Mukhtar, old man on a horse,
Who died on the gallows tortured by his wounds.
'He would have been a ghaffir now,' said one
Keen student with a sneer.
                              Omar rests now,
Thirty-three years after his death, his tomb
Built like a pink carbuncle at the edge
Of Bereniké, Euhesperides,
Benghazi – cities beckoning the wise ones
Who once found life hard, who have claimed their inheritance
Out of the salt desert, the desert, the rock,
Preserver of fallen cities, of flesh, and of oil.

54 LETTER VI

Shut up here in our houses, then, as in a prison, we were to
our regret condemned to keep this long silence.

This autumn I felt the cold in my bones when
In the fountain of Apollo the frogs were spawning.
Persephone was faceless. Above the Jebel
The thunder grumbled.

Fortune was elsewhere, ministering her mercies,
Dispensing luck to barbarians and atheists.
We on the coast repaired the aqueducts
But the water failed us.

Then winter came and the highways flooded,
Keeping us chained to our useless harbours,
Pent in by storms, letting our cattle
Wander uncared for.

Somewhere in the east the administrators filed us
Under a pile of disregarded papers.
We were forgotten, except by the hungry
Collector of taxes.

The Governor sends me a gilt-edged invitation
To celebrate the fourteenth year of independence.
There I shall see the outlandish consuls-general
Talking dog-Latin.

My cultivated friend, please try to send me
Whatever new books the sophists have published:
I have read the reviews in the six-month-old journals
And feel a provincial.

'We traded in shrouds: people stopped dying.'
Fortune frustrates even our death-wish.
The infant mortality figures were lost by
The census department.

Remember me now to my old friends and colleagues,
Discussing the Trinity and aureate diction:
Think of me here, awaiting the fires of
The Austuriani.

See where they squat behind the escarpment,
Ignorant of metre, of faction and schism,
Destined by favourless Fortune to be the true
Heirs of the Kingdom.

I am breathing an air tainted by the decay of dead bodies. I am
waiting to undergo myself the same lot that has befallen so many others.

Lethe, rock fissure, dark water, warm
Breath of white mist on drifting scum, not moving
Unless a white shape moves from rock to rock.
Nostrils drink steam, the air has shapes, can be touched,
Assumes phantoms. Drink here, drink, the brackish taste
On the roof of the mouth, closed with a green coin.
I am ready to descend, to enter the cave's mouth,
To put on the mist's habit, boarding the frail
Craft that has come to claim me.
                                          In 1938
The Lido at Lethe was opened to the public
And a poem by d'Annunzio was unveiled
Limned on a carefully ruined stele. Balbo
Offered full citizenship to all who filled in
The necessary forms. Electric cables
Illuminated the forgetful waters and
Two wrought-iron gates guarded oblivion.
Bertolo Giannoni at about this time
Managed to reach the grotto's far wall
And scratched his name in letters a metre high.
Perhaps by some irony he was one of those
Crushed by the tank-tracks of Keith Douglas's troop
On the way through to Agheila and Tripoli.
Bertolo survives on the wall, having drunk the waters.

The filth of pigeons, two fig trees' silver leaves,
Roots splayed from rock channels. Persephone in fossils.
He threw the switch and the sixty-watt bulbs flashed on
Too feebly to desecrate the pre-electric dark.
I walked on duck-boards over the breathing lake.
The mist came walking towards me.
                                          Death is a mystery
Not needing these adventitious theatricals.
In the ancient darkness the eirenic shades sleep,
Forgetting Lethe, rock fissure, dark water, warm breath.

*A camel with the mange, says the proverb, can shoulder the
burden of many asses.*

When they came to ask me to serve
We were sitting over a dish of olives, drinking
Wine from Messa, the kind that tastes of stone.
We had been talking of Constantinople, the embassy
I relished so little, so far away from home.
And then they arrived, with their wallets of documents,
Their letters and seals stowed carefully away,
Their talk of Theophilus and the weather, nervously
Waiting their chance to snare me into God's acre
Before my due time. *Divine conspiracy*,
Somebody might have called it; but *duty*
Was the burden of their discourse, that
And those filial bonds they well knew bound me
To this Pentapolis, this Libya.
                              In this land
No evangelist angled for souls, no missionaries
Humped bibles along the trade routes. The sick
Children are treated by the Adventists,
The Orthodox are visited by one priest
Whose tinny bell pierces the muezzin's cry,
The quiet white nuns herd schoolgirls here and there,
And over the dust and potholes of the town
The double-breasted cathedral sits like a presence:
Mae West or Bardot, depending on your age.
The Anglicans have 'Newmarket'
Among the officers', and their ladies', horses:
The National Anthem, punkahs from Poona, words
Hallowed in Gloucestershire and Ulster, and
Hymns of the rousing sort by Wesley and Lyte.
In this whole land there is not one Christian
With a Libyan passport.
                        So I reluctantly
Accepted what they offered: Bishop, with power
Over five crumbling cities, fortress-farms,

69

Immitigable desert. And they accepted
My wife ('better to marry than to burn'),
My doubts, my flinching from the sweat and blood
Of trinitarian dogma. Thus I stand,
Flawed but chosen, bewildered by that choice,
Uncertain of creed, fouled in a Marian web,
Deafened by Alexandrian echoes, armed
With episcopal power in a parish of termites.

                                                 Look,
At Birsis, among the rotten byres, a vaulted
Church in ruins, where a man hoes red
Soil fed with Roman water. In the rubble
A fragment shows, in frayed Greek letters, words
To the Lord, and something else I cannot read.
The servants of the Lord. Alone, he hoes and sings,
Singing to himself. Perhaps to someone else.

57   LETTER IX

*Brought up outside the pale of the Church, and having
received an alien training, I grasped at the altars of God.*

The Dalmatians have landed their advance party
And the billeting–officer is hard at work.
I can now administer the Mass in Serbo-Croat
But the congregation is thin. I carry Christ
Like a burden on my tongue. Andronicus –
From tunny fisher's perch to governor's chariot –
Is excommunicated, but runs giddy still.
My bow sprouts mould in the yard, I have given away
My dogs, my saddle.
                         Once there was philosophy
But how can that clear stream run when I spend my days
Adjudicating ruridecanal tiffs at Hydrax or Darnis,
Squabbles about copes or the laying on of hands?
Hypatia, remember the hush in the lecture-room
When you entered serenely with your astrolabe
And began to enunciate truths?

Tonight at five
A conversation-lesson with the Praetor, whose Greek
Would not fill a sardine. Yes, I am peevish.
You may say it is the climate or the place or my time of life –
But I carry a burden that was given to me
Which I do not understand. Somewhere, God's plan
Is hidden in monoliths or a wafer of bread.
His purpose obscurely works through those Slavs on the hill
As I offer his flesh and blood. Neither Gentile nor Jew
In that Kingdom. So I puzzle it out, till I hear
A knock at my study door. Come in, Praetor, come.

58 LETTER X

*And yet this is nothing but what the ancient oracle announced
as to how the Pentapolis must end.*

What the oracle said was vapour swathing the rock,
And we could discern a finger writing in steam
As on a tiled wall the obscene words
Doing death to life in hints and half-promises.
'Libya shall perish by the wickedness of its leaders.'
Unequivocal, you think, for the oracle?
The ambiguities are all ours –
Rumours of referendum, of abdication:
Denials of rumours, official circumlocutions:
Whispers in cafés, public demonstrations,
Restoration of order, and if necessary
The 2 a.m. visits, the executions.
I hear the same story twice, and pass on
A third version, atomized by now
To fragments with different names and places,
But still – substantially, you say – but still
The truth holds, and the whisperers hold to it.
The oracle grins like a toad, and belches fumes.

Battus stammered and lisped. Coming to ask for a voice,
He was bidden instead to build an empire. Oracle,
You are the echo of ignorance, though I believe you.
For 'abounding in fleeces' read 'running over with oil'.

Conspicuous waste, money's confederate,
Marks the economy's frontiers. Tin cans,
Bottles, bones, blood, uncollected
In a city without dustbins, demonstrate
How well we are doing.
                        The cities of the plain
Flourished as we do, but a belly-dancer
At the Riviera or the Berenice
Will hardly call God down with his dust and ashes.
Dust and ashes are what is native here,
Unprophesied and sempiternal. Doom
Carries a drilling-rig in a Landrover,
A geologist from Yale, and a cloud of rumour
Stinking along the salt-pans whose flamingoes
Have flown away, over whose white plateaux
The ghibli blows from the south, bringing dust to the tongue.

Andronicus, imperialist British, wily
Egyptian agitator, Zionist, Polish agent
Disguised as an engineer – you have handed over
This traduced Kingdom. Equipped for Armageddon,
The alien cavalry rides off, but in the squares
Public loudspeakers broadcast messages
Of peace, stability, spontaneous joy,
Showing how once again etcetera
And how etcetera the future is
If only we hold firm. Etcetera.

The tomb of Battus, long located here,
In fact is there. No matter. He is dead.
The archaeologists can shift him as they please.
Fires, watchtowers, fires. The oracle, asleep,
Snores in her ancient dreams, and round her head
The angels, mingling with the harpies, weep.

*War and famine have not yet annihilated it completely, as
was foredoomed; but they are wearing it away and destroying
it little by little.*

Holes in the earth, places of snakes and fleas:
We shall creep in on our bellies, we shall find refuge
Among the ignorant, the outcast, those who merit
No conquest, being too low already.
There, I suppose, we shall die.
                                    This 'resurrection'
I take as allegory, for when we die,
There, in a hole like a brood of field-mice, can you
Imagine our suffocated, wasted bodies
Assuming, in some flash of lightning, wings
To make us rise, harps to be struck for joy,
And crowns to inherit the Kingdom? The Kingdom is here.

Or here, where the woman near Sirte smiles,
Smiling with stained teeth, hands red with henna,
Holding a child whose nose is running and whose ears
Are pierced for ear-rings big as saucers.
So she smiles, accustomed, poor, expecting no change.

Long before dawn the cocks are crowing here:
Their catalogue of betrayal fills the night.
At six the sky is a dome of brilliant blue,
Only at the edges furred with a grey mist
Presaging another day of burning. Who will burn?
We are not martyrs yet, and if we are
We shall not burn but be trapped in our fastnesses,
Beyond the episcopal court, the Rood, the Grail.

Hesychius, I have seen your house, its dutiful mosaics
(Where you recorded your family and our God)
Erupting like waves from centuries of rain,
Seismic disturbance, tumult of war and anthill.
The long attrition begins, the mills of God

Grind us to dust the ghibli blusters north
Into the sea where no fleet aims to fan
With Dorian sails our northward passage home.
The woman near Sirte smiles, who is to come
After barbarians, pillage, drought; and we
Are dust in the holes of the earth and under the sea.

60 LETTER XII

I am a minister of God, and perchance I must complete my
service by offering up my life. God will not in any case overlook
the altar, bloodless, though stained by the blood of a priest.

I have reached the end. I shall write to you no more.
Dies irae is come. See the hole in heaven
The tribesmen of Cyrene showed to Battus.
I cling to the church's pillars. These are the Kingdom's last days.
Here are the stoups of holy water, here
The table of sacrifice. The victim is also here.

Set sail for Jedda or Jerusalem,
The miracles are due. Here is a splinter
They say is from the Rood, and here a flag
That has snuffed the air of Mecca. I leave myself
As an unholy relic, to be the dust
Neglected by the seller of souvenirs
Among his lamps, his bronzes, his rubbed coins.
Here by the shore God's altar is made whole,
Unvisited by celebrants, to be restored
By the Department of Antiquities.
Functional concrete (ruddled, grey, and brash)
Marks out what's lacking: marble, granite, wood,
The divine interstices.
                                        I abdicate
Having survived locust, earthquake, death
Of children, failure of crops, murrain of hopes,
And am become that ambassador in bonds
Paul spoke of.

Now the muezzin calls his first
Exhortation, and the pillars fall.
Darkness is on the Jebel, tongues of flame
Bring ruin, not revelation. See how they lick
The rod of Aaron, Zelten's oily fires
Flaring against the night. The visions come.
The pilgrims have boarded, the pagans are at my throat.
The blood of a Greek is spilt for the blood of a Jew.
Altars are stained, a lamb is dragged by its legs
To bleed at the door of the house.
                                        Libya,
Image of desolation, the sun's province,
Compound of dust and wind, unmapped acres –
This is the place where Africa begins,
And thus the unknown, vaguer than my conjectures
Of transubstantiation, Trinity,
All those arcana for which, now, I die.

from *Inscriptions*

I have hidden something in the inner chamber
And sealed the lid of the sarcophagus
And levered a granite boulder against the door
And the debris has covered it so perfectly
That though you walk over it daily you never suspect.

Every day you sweat down that shaft, seeing on the walls
The paintings that convince you I am at home, living there.
But that is a blind alley, a false entrance
Flanked by a room with a few bits of junk
Nicely displayed, conventionally chosen.
The throne is quaint but commonplace, the jewels inferior,
The decorated panels not of the best period,
Though enough is there to satisfy curators.

But the inner chamber enshrines the true essence.
Do not be disappointed when I tell you
You will never find it: the authentic phoenix in gold,
The muslin soaked in herbs from recipes
No one remembers, the intricate ornaments,
And above all the copious literatures inscribed
On ivory and papyrus, the distilled wisdom
Of priests, physicians, poets and gods,
Ensuring my immortality. Though even if you found them
You would look in vain for the key, since all are in cipher
And the key is in my skull.

The key is in my skull. If you found your way
Into this chamber, you would find this last:
My skull. But first you would have to search the others,
My kinsfolk neatly parcelled, twenty-seven of them
Disintegrating in their various ways.
A woman from whose face the spices have pushed away
The delicate flaking skin: a man whose body

Seems dipped in clotted black tar, his head detached:
A hand broken through the cerements, protesting:
Mouths in rigid grins or soundless screams –
A catalogue of declensions.

How, then, do I survive? Gagged in my winding cloths,
The four brown roses withered on my chest
Leaving a purple stain, how am I different
In transcending these little circumstances?
Supposing that with uncustomary skill
You penetrated the chamber, granite, seals,
Dragged out the treasure gloatingly, distinguished
My twenty-seven sorry relatives,
Labelled them, swept and measured everything
Except this one sarcophagus, leaving that
Until the very end: supposing then
You lifted me out carefully under the arc-lamps,
Noting the gold fingernails, the unearthly smell
Of preservation – would you not tremble
At the thought of who this might be? So you would steady
Your hands a moment, like a man taking aim, and lift
The mask.
          But this hypothesis is absurd. I have told you already
You will never find it. Daily you walk about
Over the rubble, peer down the long shaft
That leads nowhere, make your notations, add
Another appendix to your laborious work.
When you die, decently cremated, made proper
By the Registrar of Births and Deaths, given by *The Times*
Your two-inch obituary, I shall perhaps
Have a chance to talk with you. Until then, I hear
Your footsteps over my head as I lie and think
Of what I have hidden here, perfect and safe.

To reconstruct an afternoon in an antique time
Out of a broken dish, some oyster shells
And an ashy discolouration of the otherwise ochreous soil –
This is an occupation for philosophers
With more than a taste for language-problems.
It has no value beyond itself. Not even
The scrupulous cataloguing of shape, disposition, provenance
Will alleviate the strong smell of futility rising
Like a cloud of midges: the site-notebook
Is, like what it records, a disjected and maybe random
Commentary without conclusions.
                                        In a trial trench
On the excavation's southernmost flank, some young sprig
Teases a knucklebone out of a beautifully vertical
Wall, marks its cavity with a meat-skewer,
Ties to it something very like a miniature luggage-label
And drops it into a tray. Visitors observe
This performance with the set faces of persons determined
Not to be taken in; and in a sense
Their stance is a true one. Why, indeed,
Do I peer attentively at holes in roads
Or fossick about in the earth's disturbances
Or the mud of the foreshore? Imagining
Some lost groat or cup-handle will tell me
More about life than I know already,
Or simply a souvenir of luck and persistence?
I have stopped asking myself, accepting such furtive burrowings
As native to me, as mild and dim
As other people's secret traffickings.

No value, then, in these subterranean doings,
No moral to point, for once. Except I have
Some cold thought hovering here, which recognizes
The damp earthfall, the broken dish, the bone
Labelled and dropped in a tray and made to fit
In a pattern I have not guessed at yet, and may never,
But go on living with and through, no doubt.

63   *At Souillac*

Down the congested air, toothed beak and wing
Tear at each clinging couple stitched in stone:
Twisted within the whirlpool all go down
Where hooks and talons, fangs and pincers cling
Till the condemned are smothered, and they drown.

Outside, the air is warm, the light is clear,
The postcards concentrate on happier stuff
(A close-up of Isaiah is enough),
And nobody has anything to fear.
But something clings and will not let me off.

An allegory even saints condemn –
Ridiculous beasts and monsters, caricatures
Of evil doodled in the boring hours
When stonedust choked the throats of thirsty men –
Through that stone tunnel a dark torrent pours.

It breeds among the shadows, out of sight,
A chain of interlocking actions which,
As stone plaits over stone, and stitch with stitch,
Have nothing more to do with warmth and light
Than a crowned virgin stained as black as pitch.

Under the one step up into the hut
A toad broods by the sergeant's shabby boots.
A single light bulb, acid and unshaded,
Marks out, inside, a function of the state
As well as marking where one road has ended.

Slogans ('To be on guard is half the battle')
Assure the walls if not the occupants.
Only behind a door do I catch glimpses
Of cruder appetites: a brown thigh, supple
With bourgeois blandishments, coyly entices.

Ripped from some old *Paris Match* or *Playboy*,
This functionary's unofficial decor
Cheers me a little as I sit and wait
While name and date of birth and date of entry
Are slowly copied to a dossier sheet.

Outside, between the frontier posts, the hills
Are black, unpeopled. Hours of restlessness
Seep from the silence, silt across the road.
At last the sergeant puts away his files,
Hands me my papers. And I see the toad

Hop into darkness, neutral and unstopped,
Companion of the brown-thighed cover girl
Hidden behind the door, beyond the frontier,
Where appetite and nature are adept
At moving quietly, or at staying still.

65   Dead Wood

Worn down to stumps, shredded by the wind,
Crushed underfoot in brittle slaty husks,
The forest turned from wood to stone to dust.

The rind of bark peeled off in slivers, shed
Dry spores, mineral resins, scales of scrim,
Scattering huge-leaved branches under the sun.

These giants shrank to pygmies in the glare.
Basilisks flashed their petrifying eyes.
The whole plateau rattled with bones of trees.

Now oil-men bring the few gnarled timbers back
As souvenirs. A lopped stone branch lies there
To hold up books, or prop open a door.

66   At the Italian Cemetery, Benghazi

Meglio un giorno da leone che cent'anni da pecora.

                                        MUSSOLINI

The old rhetoric inflated beyond rigour,
The Roman virtues in a cloud of sand
Blown to a mirage, detonate and roar
Like the lion, extinct since Balbo pressed the trigger
In 1936, far in the south. Here
A place of cypresses, a little Italy
Grazed by the desert wind, an enclave
For the dead, for a dead colony.
Among them all, not one unpolluted grave.
Mare Nostrum is someone else's sea.

The Mediterranean was to be a lake
Round which the imperium flourished. There came
Boatloads of dialects, music, priests,
A whole army: bushels of grain,
Cattle, tractors: archaeologists to make
The past justify the present. *Hang thirty a day
And resistance will stop. Subdue and civilize.*
The sun has flaked the neat stucco away.
Sepia fades from Cesare's, from Fabbro's eyes.
The sheep are slaughtered, the lion would not stay.

White villages were built, made ready, named
Heroically or nostalgically:
D'Annunzio, Savoia, Maddalena.
Rebels were strangled, nomads gaoled and tamed.
Dutiful bells rang across jebel and plain,
Ave Marias drowning the muezzin's cry.
Calabria, Naples, Sicily put out
Frail shoots into the hot breath of the ghibli.
Duce, Duce, the parched gullets shout,
Then the bombs fall, the echoes drift and die.

Vulgar memorials, stricken and deluded:
Marble sarcophagi, vain crucifix.
Walking here, why am I now reminded
Puzzlingly of what some cynic said:
Life is a preparation
For something that never happens? The Italian dead
Are gathered under their alien cypresses,
The path gives off its dusty exhalation,
The broken arm of an angel lifts and blesses
The lion-crazed, the shepherdless, one by one.

Soldiers Plundering a Village

Down the mud road, between tall bending trees,
Men thickly move, then fan out one by one
Into the foreground. Far left, a soldier tries
Bashing a tame duck's head in with a stick,
While on a log his smeared companion
Sits idly by a heap of casual loot—
Jugs splashing over, snatched-up joints of meat.

Dead centre, a third man has spiked a fourth—
An evident civilian, with one boot
Half off, in flight, face white, lungs short of breath.
Out of a barn another soldier comes,
Gun at the ready, finding at his feet
One more old yokel, gone half mad with fear,
Tripped in his path, wild legs up in the air.

Roofs smashed, smoke rising, distant glow of fire,
A woman's thighs splayed open after rape
And lying there still: charred flecks caught in the air,
And caught for ever by a man from Antwerp
Whose style was 'crudely narrative', though 'robust',
According to this scholar, who never knew
What Pieter Snayers saw in 1632.

A souvenir from Sicily on the shelf:
A wooden doll carved out of some dark wood,
And crudely carved, for tourists. There it stood
Among the other stuff. Until one night,
Quietly reading to myself, I heard
It speak, or creak – a thin, persistent scratch,
Like the first scrape of a reluctant match,
Or unarticulated word
That made me look for it within myself

As if I talked to myself. But there it was,
Scratching and ticking, an erratic clock
Without a face, something as lifeless as rock
Until its own announcement that it shared
Our life with us. A woodworm, deep inside,
Drilled with its soft mouth through the pitch-stained wood
And like the owl presaging death of good,
Its beak closing as the dynasty died,
It held fear in those infinitesimal jaws.

So – to be practical – we must choose two ways:
Either to have some expert treat the thing
(Trivial, absurd, embarrassing)
Or throw it out, before the infection eats
The doors and floors away: this Trojan horse
In miniature could bring the whole house down,
I think to myself wildly, or a whole town . . .
Why do we do nothing, then, but let its course
Run, ticking, ticking, through our nights and days?

Day by day, day after day, we fed it
With straw, mown grass, shavings, shaken weeds,
The huge flat leaves of umbrella plants, old spoil
Left by the builders, combustible; yet it
Coughed fitfully at the touch of a match,
Flared briefly, spat flame through a few dry seeds
Like a chain of fireworks, then slumped back to the soil
Smouldering and smoky, leaving us to watch

Only a heavy grey mantle without fire.
This glum construction seemed choked at heart,
The coils of newspaper burrowed into its hulk
Led our small flames into the middle of nowhere,
Never touching its centre, sodden with rot.
Ritual petrol sprinklings wouldn't make it start
But swerved and vanished over its squat brown bulk,
Still heavily sullen, grimly determined not

To do away with itself. A whiff of smoke
Hung over it as over a volcano.
Until one night, late, when we heard outside
A crackling roar, and saw the far field look
Like a Gehenna claiming its due dead.
The beacon beckoned, fierily aglow
With days of waiting, hiding deep inside
Its bided time, ravenous to be fed.

Green bulwark of the chestnut heaves in air
Towards this window, cleaves and tosses spray
From leaf to leaf, its branched and clustered prow
Heavy under the clouds' insistent flow.
Its toppling weight flings higher than the house,
Falling and rising massively to where
A jet goes blundering, roaring on its way
Across a sky obscured with thickened boughs.

Rooted and restless, watching behind glass
Such fierce contenders harmlessly perform
Their rapt compulsions, now I turn away
And face books, papers, furniture, my day
Belittled by the sight, as if my own
Making was measured thus and could not pass
Tests so devised, or cast in such a form.
Each branch is shaken, every leaf is blown.

And so I look again, and find it now
As still and two-dimensional as some
Backcloth from *Hagoromo*, a green tree
In front of which masked men and spirits see
The pattern of their future, unperturbed
And not to be evaded. On one bough
A thrush has settled. Its clear measures come
Across clear lengths of distance, undisturbed.

And they will fall – bird, chestnut, house and all –
As surely as the rain, more quietly
Than the plane's swelling and withdrawing scream,
And gradually, like falling in a dream
Through boughs and clouds that scatter as we float
Downwards on air that holds us as we fall
Towards a landing place we never see,
Bare, treeless, soundless, cloudlessly remote.

Died, 1778: Moses Ozier, son of a woman out of her mind,
born in the ozier ground belonging to Mr Craft.

Christened with scripture, eponymously labelled,
You lie so small and shrunken in the verger's tall
Archaic writing. Born in the low water meadows
Down the end of lawns where you would be unlikely to walk
Supposing you'd ever got that far in life, no Pharaoh's daughter
Plucked you out of the bulrushes, for this was Yorkshire
And prophets had stopped being born. Your lunatic mother
Knelt in the rushes and squirmed in her brute pain,
Delivering you up to a damp punishing world
Where the ducks were better off, and the oziers wetly rustled
Sogged down in the marshland owned by Mr Craft.

It's sense to suppose you lasted a few days
And were buried, gratis, in an unmarked hole at the edge
Of the churchyard, the verger being scrupulous
And not wanting your skinny christened bundle of bones
To lie in unhallowed ground.

                Poor tiny Moses,
Your white face is a blank, anonymous
Like other people's babies. Almost two hundred years
Since you briefly lay by the cold and placid river,
And nothing but nineteen words as memorial.

I hear you cry in the night at the garden's dark edge.

Below the ford, the stream in flood
Rises and laps the leaf-choked wood
And fallen branches trap thick mud.
Pebbles are swept like slingstones down
Runnels and channels sliced through stone
And in the hollows sink and drown.

On either side broad ramparts hold
The water back from copse and field,
Where a dry earthbank seems to fold
Protectively a hollow space
Of pasture edged with stunted trees
In its inert and curved embrace.

Six hundred years ago, great pike
Grown old in this man-fashioned lake
Swam through its lily clusters like
Dream-presences below the mind.
Dark waters stirred where now I stand
Hearing the distant stream unwind.

The stillness here was made to last.
Whatever shapes survive exist
In some faint diagram of the past,
A sketch-map tentative as those
Robbed walls whose simulacrum lies
In patches summer droughts expose.

One wall still overtops the trees
Beyond the ford, but bramble grows
Round rotten stone. What energies
Persist are harnessed to the stream,
Violent in flood, not curbed or tame,
And hurtling without plan or aim.

The hazed meadows of England grow over chancels
Where cattle hooves kick up heraldic tiles
And molehills heap their spoils above slumped walls.
The cruck-beamed roofs of refectories nestle under
Sheds and barns, hay piled high where
Augustine and Aquinas chapter by chapter
Were read in these now lapsed pastoral acres.

Small streams wash the smashed crockery of Cistercians.
Stone-plaited carvings are wedged in gable ends
Of farmhouses, springs irrigate robbed chapels
Where all is marsh, reeds meshed among cracked altars.
A buzzard shrieks *yaa-i* in a tall tree,
Plainchant echoing along the valleys.
High hedges stand above spoiled finials.

And Sunday mornings see small meeting houses,
Reformed parishes and tabernacles,
Bethesdas and the whole wide countryside,
All split seven ways in sect and congregation,
Assembling to praise God from whom all blessings
Flow through his derelict priories, abbeys, cells
The afternoon sun will show, faint shadows among fields.

This sea has been going a long time,
Sluicing out gullies, chafing rocks,
Grinding boulders to pebbles, and scouring pebbles
Till the hard white veins stand out.

                              It lifts its wet tons
Heavily from the low fathoms, it makes nonsense
Of timbers and lobster-pots, it polishes bottles
To frivolous bits of glitter, goes eating on
Through cliffs and headlands, thudding its steady fist
Into igneous layers gone cold after eruptions,
And the litter of low coasts is like confetti to it.

Tides don't tame it, the moon knows that,
Pulling and pushing with a slow, drugged rhythm:
They can't stop those pools and pockets swarming with its fry
When the great thing itself is almost out of sight
Flicking and flickering on the horizon –
It's coming back, it's gathering its windy breath
To stride back up its beaches, to knock again
Heavily hammering at its lost sea-bed
Now calling itself America or Europe,
Names to be carried awhile, till they tumble back
Into the boiling mess that started it all,
Hot seas without vessels, coasts, rocks, fish,
Unmapped, ungovernable, without tidy names.

Elsewhere, the autumn wood fills with red leaves
Silently. Worm-casts spill across meadows.
Grass withers. The sun moves west, assigning cold.

Elsewhere, a magpie clacks into the trees.
A kestrel treads on air. The path is thick
With turfed-out snail-shells, and against a gate

A squirrel hangs as hostage. Elsewhere, too,
Smoke drifts across valleys, blossoms above towns
Invested by artillery. Along highways

Drivers hurry to suburbs where lawns lie
Heavy under rain, unmown. Elsewhere children
Are rawly born. And the moon inclines its light

On domes, torn posters, curfew guards. Elsewhere,
You sit on a bed while across the corridor
A scream spirals and jerks, again, again,

Then spins down fast and settles into sobs.

And no elsewhere is here, within your head
Where nothing else is born, or grows, or dies.
Nothing is like this, where the world turns in

And shapes its own alarms, noises, signs,
Its small aggressions and its longer wars,
Its withering, its death. Outside, begins

Whatever shape I choose to give it all
(Clouds ribbed with light, signals I recognize)
But you sit silent, narrowly, in a world

So light I feel it brush my cheek, and fall.

76 Dead Metaphors

A child refusing to be born, carried so long
It smothers the heart, dying as the mother dies.
A scar speaking in cold weather of the flesh it was.
A purlieu of levelled bricks where a house once stood.
A hand reaching out in the dark and closing on nothing.
A stain washed faint, neither wine nor blood.

And it is not a child, because we never met,
Nor is it a scar, because no wound was there,
Nor is it waste ground, because in the empty air
No house was ever built, and our hands were closed like fists
Keeping what we had, and whatever we spilt
Gathers like dry stuff a vague girl dusts.

77 Switzerland

In a valley in Switzerland a brass band marches.
The dapper chalets twinkle in the sun
Among the meadows and the well-drilled larches
And watercourses where streams briskly run.

Bravely the little drums pretend their thunder
To far-off crags whose melting snow brings down
A rattle of small pebbles buried under
Drifts deeper than the church spire in the town.

The soldier-citizens of the canton practise
Before an audience of sheep and cows.
As for the real thing, the simple fact is
Each keeps a well-oiled rifle in his house.

Duchies and principalities have fathered
These drums and cornets under angrier skies,
Bucolic bellicosities which gathered
The Ruritanian airs of paradise

Into a clockwork joke envious Europe
Could laugh at, play in, patronize, ignore,
As, poised between the saddle and the stirrup,
The Switzer was acknowledged as a bore.

The peaceable kingdom rests on marks and dollars
Beside the lake at Zurich, lined with banks,
Far from the towns draped with insurgent colours
Whose dawn breaks with the grinding tread of tanks.

The Alpine avalanche holds back this summer
Its fragile tons, and watches from the height
The nimble piper and the strutting drummer
Putting the valley's herbivores to flight.

78 *Now*

So many of them, and so many still to come:
They crowd the pavements, pour from the discreet chimneys
Of crematoria, advance with arms linked
Down avenues, protesting or celebrating,
Are spaded under sand and rock and clay,
And still come young and bloodily among us.
It will go on, nothing can stop it happening

Given that first great sunburst, and the mindless time
Moving towards cell and union, coelacanth and midge,
What could prevent sparse tribes of hominids
Drifting like winged seeds over the land-masses
And ending up here, on the second floor
Of a house facing south, one Sunday in October,
Caught in the middle years and counting syllables?

79   Generation Gap

Outside, on the dark campus lawns,
An apoplectic howling goes
On and on, while inside dons
Sit glumly listening to the news
In nordic-brutalist maisonettes.

Outside, the grammar-school head boy
Now on a trip to God-knows-where
Shrieks for ten demons to destroy
The demons tearing his fuzzed hair.
The nuclear family goes to bed.

And quiet at last, as midnight comes,
The lowland mists creep through the grass
Towards the functional dark rooms
And leave a cloud upon the glass
That lasts till daylight, and beyond.

80   *Inscriptions*

Knickers Fisher has been at work again,
Using a compass point on the closet door,
But he's a miniaturist whose main concern
Is altogether different from the team
Exhibiting on the wall by the railway line:
SMASH THE STATE stands six feet high or more
In strong black paint where the track crosses the stream –
Opposites in the field of graphic design.

And in the middle scale are the stone slabs
Pecked out by masons dead these hundred years,
Gravestones along the passage to the town:
They make their claims too, with a different voice,
But still in hope and expectation. They
Exhort and yearn and stiffly mask the fears
Of men with large obsessions and small choice,
Burdened with flesh and law till judgement day.

81 *A Haiku Yearbook*

Snow in January
Looking for ledges
To hide in unmelted.

February evening:
A cold puddle of petrol
Makes its own rainbow.

Wind in March:
No leaves left
For its stiff summons.

April sunlight:
Even the livid bricks
Muted a little.

Wasp in May
Storing his venom
For a long summer.

Morning in June:
On the sea's horizon
A white island, alone.

July evening:
Sour reek of beer
Warm by the river.

August morning:
A squirrel leaps and
Only one branch moves.

September chestnuts:
Falling too early,
Split white before birth.

October garden:
At the top of the tree
A thrush stabs an apple.

November morning:
A whiff of cordite
Caught in the leaf mould.

Sun in December:
In his box of straw
The tortoise wakes.

This is the arrow which I, a warrior, shot,
Lifting up the bow-end:
Let it remind those who find it
To talk of me for ever.
                KASA KANAMURA (fl. A.D. 715–33)

                        I

At the Yoshino Palace, in the fifth month,
Kasa Kanamura, laureate of Nara,
Anthology compiler, brocaded and pale,
Lifted the supple bow, drew breath,
Drew back the bowstring with the bamboo arrow
And smoothly let flow forth the tip of bright metal.

It lay where it fell, away from the target,
And lay as he left it.
                He, struck (like no target)
With the thought of it lying
Where it had fallen
To stay there . . . And so
'I, a warrior' flowed smooth from his brush
On the scroll before him, as he fingered the syllables
And spoke without breath
And walked to his grave,
Who had seen the quick torrents
Shouldering the mountains
And the tumbling cascades
Race by the palace
(Stout-timbered, stone-walled) and
'In dread of their majesty'
Had sunk in his mind
To the rock-bed below,
And had stood, his mind floating
Like Mitsune after him . . .
Arrow, bright arrow
Fallen, there.

II

Fluted like this one, no longer than the first joint
Of my little finger, the bright bronze burnished
Under the weathers of twelve hundred years:
And not among grave goods, with cuirass and bracelet
Or gilded helmet or suppliant vessels,
But lodged in the thick grass of a humid summer
To lie under plaited leaves, under welts of mud,
Pressed down, trodden under, lost where it landed
In a curve out of air from bow, gut, pressure
Of fingers against arc of muscle, of air . . .

III

Today is the anniversary
Of Gamae, Nasamonian, one who ate locusts
And slept in the tombs of his ancestors
So as to dream prophecies:
Today such a man died
Somewhere in the desert north of the Psylli
Who were buried as they marched
To vanquish the South Wind.

And today, too, the anniversary
Of Arx, miner of obsidian,
Who lugged the black nuggets from a cliff on Lipari
To be fashioned by other men: and of Oyu,
Carver of bone amulets in Hokkaido:
Of Tacan, acolyte, of Chichen Itza – all
Inventions, you take it rightly, type-names of the nameless
Whose artefacts are numbered, labelled, filed
In corridors, in dustless libraries,
Mapped by distribution, plotted by computer,
Under whose alluvial tonnage the nostrils drew in air
And suffocated at the mortal touch.

Humbled among trophies, mementoes not only of death.

IV

At Karnak the lintels
At Thebes the pediments
At Antioch the walls
At Nineveh the pavements
At Konarak the platforms
At Sidon the bollards
At Troy the columns
At Angkor the terraces . . .
Yoshino fallen, the thousand ages
Drawn to the point of the tip of an arrow.

V

And at Augila the dates
The salt hills gushing water
And the crying of women
And Ghirza buried:
Acreage of stones
Above wells of water
And a flake of volcano
Flashing black fire,
Worked with the thumb
Shaped into sharpness
The tooth of the serpent
Hardened to stone
The flail of the scorpion
Petrified, polished

The armature perished
The poison crushed
To crystals of dust.

VI

In the palm of my left hand
Among the unread lines
The arrowhead lies cupped:
Its point, still sharp, defines

Its purpose, its abrupt
Quiddity. To end
Function is not to kill,
Nor lack of it to die.
The thousand ages cram
Survival's narrow way
With fragments. What I am
Emerges from the rubble.

VII

A topography of debris – clay, stone, bronze –
Dry hills of Mamelukes, Ghadames slagheaps,
The tells of Troy, the tip of Aberfan,
The mounds and spills at boundaries, beyond limits,
Smoking like Golgotha
                        as the ash descends
Sealing the thrown waste, the scoured junk,
Burying the scourings, embalming the long lost.
                            No sudden blast of cobalt
In the revelations of August, the fleshprint
                             shadowed on stone
As ghost presence, instant eidolon, but
A longer dying, a protracted chapter
Of accidents and discarded product:
The slaughter of utensils, the annihilation of weapons,
Carcases of tools, scattering of stones,
Lifted into the air by the grovelling shovel, and held
Here in the obsolete point that missed the target to
'Remind those who find it
                        to talk of me forever.'

VIII

And so it does,
Though not as you meant it,
Not knowing beyond Nara
The islands and mountains
Or seeing forever

Stretch to this point. Yet
Your poem contains
Its own assurance,
A blind inheritance
We share, in going on
Because we must,
Surviving destruction,
Valuing the dust.

from *New Confessions*

The reticulations of the centipede
The ripe haze of the clogged orchard
The brief gamut of rain sounding in gutters
The moss still warm in the quail's empty lair
The thin crushed touch of gravel to the nostrils
The spectrum smeared on the narrow paths of snails
The wind heaving the canvas and bracing it taut
The pierced arrow from which stormclouds bleed light
The nipple rising in its stippled disc –

                                                    Ask
What binds them in perfection, each perfect,
Distinct in harmony, joined in separation,
Poised to admit, administer, reject,
Supple in passiveness, precise in action . . .

                                                Question
How each maintains its place, follows its destiny
Through maze of choice, through labyrinth of error,
Unhindered in its rapt scrutiny
Of its own selfhood in its selfhood's mirror . . .

                                                Enquire
What chooses each one's scale and range, duration
In centuries or seconds, when each dies
Or each gives birth, where bounds are set to function
And how something of each survives and stays . . .

                                            Then praise
Your scrupulous, enquiring ignorance
That weighs, notates, equates and calculates
Through instrument and seminar to advance
Knowledge compounded of ciphers, digits, dates,
Curves of progression, graphs of incidence,
Footnotes to texts, glosses to notes on notes –
And in the end, triumphant, shrugs to advance
The notion that all this depends on chance,
A blizzard of randomness where each separate flake
Whirls in its own six-sided snowy quake,
Starting from nothing, ending in nothing, blank

As untouched drifts of snow, without meaning till
Footprints mark out the power of man's will:
Neat as the rhyme in perfect measured lines,
Technique ascends, the universe declines
To fall through holes in space that no one knew
Existed till professors told them to . . .

The reticulations of the centipede
Move effortlessly, thriftily, at speed.

84 *XXXV*

Your vigilante brother
Is full of pious deeds.
He'll take his Catholic mother
And scourge her till she bleeds
Because her father's father
Was maybe short on faith
And possibly would rather
Have saved his mortal breath
Than stand with sixty others
In the hallelujah tent
Shouting to a God that bothers
About what Donatus meant.
O the wicked sins of the mothers
O the temple veil is rent.

Your vigilante stalwart
Enjoys himself at night.
Tying a rope true-love knot
May seem a mild delight,
But your vigilante ties it
Round necks and pulls it till
The victim chokes and cries 'It
Is true about God's Will!',

After which the poor old sinner
May have a moment's peace
Before a sword is in her
And she's bleeding on her knees.
O the true Lord is a winner
O God's Adversary flees.

'Now gather round, my bullies,'
Your vigilante cries.
'We must revenge old follies,
And he who wavers dies.
Up with the true religion,
Up with the holy books,
The dove is not our pigeon,
Carry daggers in your looks.
For wasn't it Our Lord himself
Who said he brought not peace
But a sword – so take it off the shelf
And give your souls release.'
O judge what's true, each for himself
O you who joy in peace.

85 XXXVII

No one had told me this was what to expect:
The mouth full of ashes, still warm from the promised feast,
And the slivers of bone hacked from the offered beast
And the dry knot in my gullet not wanting to swallow.
No one told me. Released
From condign ambitions, from words of a worldly text,
I stand on this spit of sand, pointing north from home,
Stale spit sour in my mouth, the devils brought low
In front across tracts of livid disordered foam
And behind across still deserts, unsettlable waste.

Without dignity, without position
Except to keep upright, propped between day and night,
The refugees crowd wanly out of sight:
But I know they are there, unsummoned to the feast,
Without fire, without light,
In attitudes of abandon or contrition.
They have suffered: suffer: the losers, they pay
For their leaders' heresy, the mark of the beast
Branded yesterday, confirmed today
To go on suffering, until proved contrite.

Carthage, you too were brought low, garnished with salt,
A triumph of waste, defaced for your impudence.
I have seen our enemies burned for their vile offence,
Should find it just, should applaud the divinity
That has wrung the due expense
Out of that proven vileness. Scrupulous to a fault,
I measure the given word against the deed
And find the blistered child on its mother's knee
Wrings something out beyond justice: makes me bleed
For something unassurable, for innocence.

But I am committed. I accepted the thorny crown,
The stigma of blood, the word in the desert, the thrall
Banishing all but the doctrine that those who fall
Fall through the truculent will, gone wild and free.
There is no parable
Our Lord told that has set these scruples down
As I would wish them. Committed to this war,
I must accept devout belligerency.
And yet as the desert winds and the waves roar
Across this headland, I pray for some sure call
To deafen our hymns, to rise and drown us all.

I take it up and read it, and I see
Ink and papyrus melt under my gaze.
The verses blur, the luminous syllables
Lapse into darkness. In these latter days
The hills like a broken comb against the light
Scratch at each dawn and dusk, a restless music
Compounded with cicadas, crickets, flies,
Frettings of grasshoppers, the viper's hushed
Swarm down the walls and conduits: siftings, poised
As this whole town is poised, on the edge of silence.

From floor to ceiling, penitential psalms
Repeat their abject praises. Thou, Lord, art just
But justice will be done among men too,
And out beyond the walls and out at sea
Our judges gather to administer it.
Nevertheless, Thy will be done: the church
Fills with your citizens, who will not hear
My voice again, which forty years have brought
To this thin whisper. Silence claims me too.
The shelves of manuscripts entomb my tongue.

The sharp prow rose and fell into the sun,
Carrying me busily on Christ's brisk errands.
Heretics fell in disputation, laws
Were balanced on the scales of my regard.
Now at the jetty no craft waits for me
Or anyone. Again I lift the book,
And close my eyes, and see a city rise
Above all brick and marble ones. Below,
Where men are fearful and their fear is just,
A gorgon mouth yawns open and breathes fire.

from *A Portion for Foxes*

87   The Unnameable

It creeps away to die, like animals,
But does not die. It burrows in the thick
Compost at ends of gardens, fetches up
Pecking at attic skylights, with the lock
Turned tight with rust, unable to escape.
It frets and rustles, uttering frail calls.

Nothing can heal or help it. Seek it out,
It will go deeper, further. It won't want
Your rescue or your comfort, knowing best
What finds may ferret out, what cures may kill.
You recognize the sounds, you smell the scent:
More, you too crouch in darkness, where an animal
Crawls on all fours, head down, the collapsing tunnel.

88   The Procession

And when you have waited there so patiently
And at last the great procession passes by
With those sad, slow tunes you hummed interminably,
How will you join them? Will you somehow try
To draw attention with a slogan scratched
Hurriedly on a bit of paper, sound
A trumpet from the window where you watched,
Hope that by standing by you will be found
Among the million others? None of these.
No matter how confused and large the crowd,
Or how well-disciplined and separate
Those solemn marchers, you will step with ease
Down from the jostling pavement, be allowed
To join them. And you will not hesitate.

89 By the Sluice

It pulses like a skin, at dusk
Is shaken like dusty silk. The current moves
But takes its impetus and gathers speed
Only beyond the sluice-gate. Here, the faint
Shudders, the morse of water almost trapped,
Perform half mesmerized, half dying too.

Yet are not dying: those trembling dots, those small
Reverberations, rise from what is hidden –
Scatters of minnows, nervous hair–triggered fry –
Grasping at sustenance, grabbing at what is given,
Submerged ferocities, brute delicacies.

What have I hidden here, or let go, lost,
With less to come than's gone, and so much gone?
Under the gate the river slams its door.

90 Metamorphosis

Something is changing.
                        Soft fold on fold of flesh
Loosen, go liquid, swell, are filled with sighing.
The moistened petals melt into a cud,
Are eaten and renewed, let down their rain
Somewhere above, are salt as sea or blood.
The wound opens, closes, aches again.

The body's instruments, the choir of love,
Tremble and falter; stumbling, become one,
Singing of such an ecstasy as can move
Habitual gestures or inert repose
Into the dance of animals, the groan
Dashed from the dropping petals of a rose
As thorns thrust stiffly in a summer wind,
And pulse and impulse, leaping, fall behind.

It was wide, true, but no wider than the straits:
Most of it boulders and pebbles, the water itself
An uneven grey-blue snake, writhing in bursts
Here and there, but elsewhere sluggish with puddles.
It was not the size of that river, or the distance they'd come,
Or the men dead with delirium, or those killed in battle,
Or the exhaustion of a long campaign. But was it
Fear of the mountains rising red from the plain,
Fear of the unknown tribes on the other side?

                                                    No,
However the legends go, or the histories patch it together,
The place was not ready. Over the other side,
Whatever travellers had come in their ones and twos
Over the centuries, was a possible paradise,
Untouched, immaculate, the dreamt-of place
(Though not for those who lived there: it never is).
We hesitate at those portals, whether Greek or Jew,
Bond or free, freethinker or devout, and are quiet
When, for a moment, history comes to a stop.
The regimental commanders muttered together; the battalions
                                                    rested;
The leader was informed.
The bend of the river waited, and went on waiting.
The mountains, the buzzards, the plain, and the other side
Waited. The signal was given.

Then they turned back.

92   *A Moment in the South*

How different the day when the great composer
Arrived with carriages in the white piazza,
Advanced through avenues of oleander
To where his willing host, full-bearded patron
Of ancient lineage, greeted him on the loggia.

This was the place (the genius knew at once)
Where he would set that awkward second act:
A hanging garden under which the gulf
Spanned sun and haze in a long breadth of blue.
Such was his exclamation to the Count.

The tourists' brochure throbs with reverence
At this munificent and thrilling scene,
Enacted among fragrant southern trees,
When in the white piazza old men sat
Watching the dust rise from those carriages.

93   *At the Ironmonger's*

To: Messrs Trew, 12 sets no. 2 Domes of Silence, 8p per set . . .

Cabinet-hinges, casement-fasteners,
Mirror-clips and drugget-pins,
Ball-catches and bale-latches,
Curtain-hooks and curtain-rings,
Brass cabin hooks and brass escutcheons,
Cotter-keys and trammel-wedges
And, in the bottom drawer,
The domes of silence.

Coffin, casket, mausoleum,
Headstone, crucifix, monumental
Lettering etched in Latin, Hebrew,
R.I.P., Kyrie Eleison,
Sword of faith and star of David,
Ritual pyre and epicedium
And, in the bottom drawer,
The domes of silence.

94   *Stereoscope:1870*

A trick of cinematic archaeology,
A wooden toy to gaze in, among views
Where rigidly the poses now amuse
A casual audience that gasps to see
How three-dimensional such people were,
With different clothes and different hair, but all
Clear in their different rooms as we are. Tall
Men lean on mantelpieces; children stir,
Or seem to stir, restless at nursery tea;
A wife works at her crochet in a chair:
And all live in a world at which we stare
Because we recognize perspective, see
How everything is close or distant, not
Smoothed to the level pages of a book.
It is at that we almost dread to look,
Such depths, such closeness, rooted to the spot.
Peer through these eyepieces: the past goes round
Like mill-sails turning where no breezes blow,
And where we were a hundred years ago
Tugs us as something lost, not to be found,

Or sought elsewhere a hundred years from now.

'Increasingly our attention is being drawn
To carvings set up to the Veteres.
(We give the word thus, though singular occurs
As much as plural: masculine and feminine
Forms have been found indifferently.
The spelling, too, varies enormously.)
We take it these mysterious deities
May be equated with the equally
Mysterious triads known by Dr Ross
As *genii cucullati*, "the cloaked gods",
Whose distribution also runs across
The northern frontier.'

          My attention nods
Over the pamphlet and the photographs
Of rough-hewn altars, each one posed and lit
As if some cack-thumbed Michelangelo,
Possessed – though self-taught and illiterate –
By things outside himself, should this way show
His genius to a universe that laughs
At transcendental posturings like these:
'To the Gods, the Veteres . . .'

          Under my eyes
Carved word and image flow together, merge,
Spreading across the scholar's cautious prose
To reach the dark rim of the very edge
That lies beyond the window's frontier:
Where Paul in Athens stooped to read the words
Inscribed upon the superstitious stone,
'To the Unknown God', and felt a moment's fear,
Possessed neither by Christ's words nor his own.

In a fading light, working towards evening,
Knowing next day the contractors will be there,
Impatient earth-movers, time-is-money men,
And the trench, hastily dug, already crumbling
(No leisure for revetments), you're suddenly aware
Of some recalcitrant thing, as when your pen
Stubs at the page
And slips stubbornly, tripped by a grease-spot, dry
Shadow-writing. The trowel hits the edge,
Solid against solid, perhaps pottery,
Perhaps bone, something curved and flush
With earth that holds it smooth as yolk in white
And both within their shell. Feel round it, go
Teasing its edges out, not in a rush
Of treasure-hunting randomness, but quite
Firmly yet tactfully, with a patient slow
Deliberation, down
Round the bounding line that holds it, up
Its cupped outline (grey or brown?
The light is bad), letting the soil slip
Smoothly away. Too quick in your eagerness
And you'll fracture its flimsy shape, be left with scraps.
What are these folds on it? A skull's brow-ridges,
Lugs at a pot-rim? Let your hand caress
Its texture, size and mass, feel for the gaps
That may be there, the tender buried edges
Held by the earth.
Now what you want is time, more time, and light,
But both are going fast. You hold your breath
And work only by touch, nothing in sight
Except the irrelevant spots of distant stars
Poised far above your intent groping here.
Exasperated, suddenly sensing how
Absurd your concentration, your hand jars
The obstinate thing; earth falls in a damp shower;

You scrabble to save it, swearing, sweating. Now,
In the total dark,
You know it's eluded you, broken, reburied, lost,
That tomorrow the bulldozers will be back;
The thing still nameless, ageless; the chance missed.

97   *Witch Bottles*

Tiger-striped or leopard-spotted – thus
The usual label of the connoisseur:
But more like a toad's metallic mottling,
And having that granular coldness.
There is a heaviness, something of the earth.

Found in London clay, ten feet down,
Or on Thames mud in fragments, sloughed skins,
Nothing so sinister there. It's when they squat
Under some old cottage's hearth or threshold,
Revealed by the wreckers, that they chill the air.

The mask, with its hourglass mouth, runs with sand
And in its belly rusty pins transfix
A chopped-out felt heart, musty in its faint
Stink of phosphate, mingling plucked hair and piss.
Charmless, a talisman exposed and shrunk

To this coagulated baleful mass:
Corroded brass, nail parings, thorns, the scum
Gathering and thickening, and now dispersed.
Somewhere a gaunt crone shrieked in the fire's heart,
Grey flesh annealed to stone, its smeltings here.

98 At Ely

John Tiptoft, Earl of Worcester, d. 1470

Among the floating passengers below
This starry lantern, hale in effigy
Tiptoft lies by his brides, immaculate:
Serene and resurrected trinity.

Restored by art, cosmetic in his grace,
Watch him embrace the pure November chill,
Who at another time, alone, knelt down
And felt the axe descend on Tower Hill.

99 Eccles

Cliffs sifting down, stiff grassblades bent,
Subdued, and shouldering off thick sand,
Boulders – compacted grout and flint –
Jut from a stranded beach, a land
Adhering thickly to the sea.
Tide-drenched, withdrawn, and drowned again,
Capsized, these buttresses still strain
Towards perpendicularity.

The place-name mimes the fallen church,
Abbreviated, shrunk to this
Truncated word, echo of speech,
A Latin ghost's thin obsequies
Carried by wind, answered by sea –
Ecclesia: the syllables
Curtailed, half heard, like tongueless bells
From empty steeples endlessly.

He crossed the dry ford and the rock-strewn course
Coming towards the city: Taxila.
Behind him, to the West, a slow loss
Of blood, not his, a show of open wounds
Not yet to be healed. He had come so far
Language had left him: he conversed in signs,
And heard replies in meaningless grunts, rough sounds,
Yelps and choked gutturals, as a dog that whines
Under a bully's blows.

                How could he bring the word
To aliens like these? What wordless miracle
Could his dubiety raise and reveal?
Practical skills, the trade of strain and stress,
The palpable structure planned in wood and stone —
These were his passport. He had come so far
Commissioned and professional: the king's messengers
Insisted on his foreign competence,
His smart outlandishness. A palace, wrought
Out of daedalian magnificence . . .
He passed between the city walls, alone,
Trusting his still invisible harbinger,
And found the king.

              The man who wanted proof
And touched those dripping hands, that leaking sore,
Laid out his stylus and his plans before
A king of men, and pitched the palace roof
High up in heaven, a mansion without walls,
Unprovable, unseen, where the rooftree falls
Down to its cloudy base, its starry floor.

Psalm 63: 10

One streaked across the road in front of us
At night – a big-brushed grey one, almost a wolf
I liked to think – somewhere in the Punjab,
Close to a village where no doubt it scavenged.
And then back home, in England,
To see what our cat brings in –
The heads of sparrows,
A mole's pink paws, the black and marbled innards
Torn from a rat, a moorhen's claws:
Rejected spoils, inedible souvenirs,
A portion for foxes.

But here there are few foxes, no wolves,
No vultures shuffling scraggily in treetops,
No buzzards drifting in sunlight, or jackal wailing
At the edge of the compound. Only a ginger cat,
Ferociously domestic, stalking the meadows
For small and lively prey, far from those borders
Where 'fall by the sword' is no Sunday metaphor
Echoed antiphonally down gentle arches,
Where even now the gleam on a raised blade
Brings back the unspeakable, the mounds of fallen
Lying in lanes, in ditches, torn, dismembered,
A sacrifice to the wrathful god, or gods:
A portion for foxes.

102 *Marriages*

How dumb before the poleaxe they sink down,
Jostled along the slaughterer's narrow way
To where he stands and smites them one by one.

And now my feet tread that congealing floor,
Encumbered with their offal and their dung,
As each is lugged away to fetch its price.

Carnivorous gourmets, fanciers of flesh,
The connoisseurs of butcher-meat – even these
Must blanch a little at such rituals:

The carcasses of marriages of friends,
Dismemberment and rending, breaking up
Limbs, sinews, joints, then plucking out the heart.

Let no man put asunder . . . Hanging there
On glistening hooks, husbands and wives are trussed:
Silent, and broken, and made separate

By hungers never known or understood,
By agencies beyond the powers they had,
By actions pumping fear into my blood.

103 *Spool*

Envy and sloth, envy and sloth:
The two-pronged pincer and the shortened breath,
The sour mouthful, the finished youth.

On the empty platform, in the full sun,
The chattering accusations begin,
And begin again, and begin again.

Too late now for the Grand Tour,
Canals and villas in the blue air.
All journeys end on the way here.

Scratching such words on an envelope,
There is nothing to capture, nothing to keep,
And the words revolve on a loop of tape:

Saying envy and sloth, envy and sloth,
The two-pronged pincer and the shortened breath,
The sour mouthful, the finished youth.

104   'Life and Other Contingencies'*

Here is the set text – neat tabulations,
The bracketed asides of algebra.

Not that I understand them, but formulas exist:
The actuary tells you what they are.

At age 46, this and this are known.
Building societies have experience.

What happened earlier will recur, given
Similar circumstances. It's common sense.

Two volumes on the shelf. Now take them down:
Open at any page, at any line.

Portions of me are money. What I leave
Will prove the logic, confirm the whole design.

What cannot be accounted for is not
The text's concern. It tells you what is what.

*By P. F. Hooker F.I.A., and L. H. Longley-Cook M.A., F.I.A.,
F.C.A.S., A.S.A., Cambridge University Press, two vols.

105   'Tell it Slant'

Precisely enigmatic. So
You draw the line: scrupulous words
Draping the naked mysteries.

Take care not to let them go.
Thoughts rise like startled birds.
Fall back on the histories.

Meticulous runes. A fearful hint
Suggested in what is not said.
Move warily among the dead.
Strike a dry spark from a flint.

Truth is partial. Name the parts
But leave the outline vague and blurred.

Mistress of passion, master of arts —
Degrees won from a cheated word.

106   Simple Poem

I shall make it simple so you understand.
Making it simple will make it clear for me.
When you have read it, take me by the hand
As children do, loving simplicity.

This is the simple poem I have made.
Tell me you understand. But when you do
Don't ask me in return if I have said
All that I meant, or whether it is true.

I like this more than that.
That is better than this.
This means this and that.
That is what this one wrote.
This is not that at all.
This is no good at all.
Some prefer this to that
But frankly this is old hat.
That is what Thissites call
Inferior this, and yet
I hope I have shown you all
That that way lies a brick wall
Where even to say 'Yes, but . . .'
Confuses the this with the that.

Instead, we must ask 'What is this?'
Then, 'Is that *that* sort of this,
Or a modified this, or a miss
As good as a mile, or a style
Adopted by that for this
To demonstrate thisness to those
Who expect a that-inclined prose
Always from this one – a stock
Response from readers like these.'
But of course the whole thing's a trick
To make you place *them* among those
Who only follow their nose,
Who are caught on the this/that spike
But who think they know what they like.

Dannie Abse, Douglas Dunn,
Andrew Waterman, Thom Gunn,
Peter Redgrove, Gavin Ewart,
Susan Fromberg Schaeffer, Stewart
Conn, Pete Brown, Elizabeth
Jennings, Jim Burns, George MacBeth,
Vernon Scannell, Edwin Brock,
Philip Hobsbaum, Fleur Adcock,
Brian Patten, Patricia Beer,
Colin Falck, David Rokeah,
Peter Dale and David Gill,
David Holbrook, Geoffrey Hill,
David Gascoyne and John Hewitt,
William Empson and Frank Prewett,
Norman Hidden, David Wright,
Philip Larkin, Ivan White,
Stephen Spender, Tom McGrath,
dom silvester houédard,
A. Alvarez, Herbert Lomas,
D.M., R.S., Donald Thomas,
Causley, Cunningham, Wes Magee,
Silkin, Simmons, Laurie Lee,
Peter Jay, Laurence Lerner,
David Day, W. Price Turner,
Peter Porter, Seamus Deane,
Hugo Williams, Seamus Heane-
y, Jonathan Green, Nina Steane,
C. Busby Smith and F. Pratt Green,
Fullers both and Joneses all,
Donald Davie, Donald Hall,
Muldoon, Middleton, Murphy, Miller,
Tomlinson, Tonks, Turnbull, Tiller,
Barker, Brownjohn, Blackburn, Bell,
Kirkup, Kavanagh, Kendrick, Kell,
McGough, Maclean, MacSweeney, Schmidt,
Hughes (of Crow) and (of *Millstone Grit*),
Sir John Waller Bt. and Major Rook,

Ginsberg, Corso, Stanley Cook,
Peter Scupham, John Heath-Stubbs,
Fenton, Feinstein, both the Grubbs,
Holloway G., Holloway J.,
Anselm Hollo and Peter Way,
Logue, O'Connor, Kevin Crossley-
Holland, Hollander, Keith Bosley,
Matthew Mead and Erica Jong,
Henry Reed and Patience Strong,
Kunitz, Kizer, Kops, Mark Strand,
Creeley, Merwin, Dickey and
The other Dickeys, Eberhart,
Bunting, Wantling, Pilling, Mart-
in Booth, a Dorn and then a Knight,
A Comfort following on a Blight,
Skelton (not the Rector of Diss –
The Poet's Calling Robin, this),
Alistair Elliot, Alastair Reid,
Michael Longley, Michael Fried,
Ian Hamilton (twice – the Scot
With 'Finlay' at the end, and the other not),
Adrians Henri, Mitchell, Stokes,
Lucie-Smith and Philip Oakes,
Father Levi of the Soc-
iety of Jesus, Alan Ross,
Betjeman, Nicholson, Grigson, Walker,
Pitter, Amis, Hilary Corke, a
Decad of Smiths, a Potts and a Black,
Roberts Conquest, Mezey, Graves and Pack,
Hugh MacDiarmid (C. M. Grieve's
His real name, of course), James Reeves,
Hamburger, Stallworthy, Dickinson, Prynne,
Jeremy Hooker, Bartholomew Quinn,
Durrell, Gershon, Harwood, Mahon,
Edmond Wright, Nathaniel Tarn,
Sergeant, Snodgrass, C. K. Stead,
William Shakespeare (no, he's dead),
Cole and Mole and Lowell and Bly,
Robert Nye and Atukwei Okai,
Christopher Fry and George Mackay

Brown, Wayne Brown, John Wain, K. Raine,
Jenny Joseph, Jeni Couzyn,
D. J. Enright, J. C. Hall,
C. H. Sisson and all and all . . .
What is it, you may ask, that Thwaite's
Up to in this epic? Yeats'
Remark in the Cheshire Cheese one night
With poets so thick they blocked the light:
'No one can tell who has talent, if any.
Only one thing is certain. We are too many.'

109   *A Girdle Round the Earth*

'King Rear was foorish man his girls make crazy'
Says something certainly about the play.
'Prutus fall on sord for bolitical reason'
Is unambiguous, though not the way
We native-speakers might have put it, who share
A language with the undoubted global poet.
In Tokyo or Benghazi, he abides
Our questioning syllabus still, will never stay
For an answer as the candidates all stare
Into the glossaried cryptograms he hides.

O Saku Seppiya, Shakhs Bey-er, O you
Who plague the schools and universities
From Patagonia to Pakistan,
From Thailand to Taiwan, how would it please
Your universal spirit to look down
And see the turbans and burnouses bent
Above your annotated texts, or see
Simplified Tales from Lamb by slow degrees
Asphyxiate the yellow and the brown?
To pick up the quotation, 'thou art free' –

But Matthew Arnold, schools inspector, who
Saw you 'self-school'd, self-scann'd', could not have known
How distantly from Stratford and the Globe
With British Council lecturers you've flown:
Midsummer Nights in Prague and Kathmandu,
Polonius stabbed dressed in a gallabiyah,
Shylock the Palestinian refugee,
And Hamlet's father's Serbo-Croat groan,
Dunsinane transported to Peru,
Kabuki for All's Well, Noh for King Lear.

'To be or not to be. Is that a question?'
The misquotations littering the page,
The prose translations fingermarked with sweat,
You prove again, world-wide, 'not of an age
But for all time', the English Ala' ad-Din,
The Western Chikamatsu, more than both
And different from either, somehow worth
Those sun-baked hours in echoing lecture-halls,
On torn tatami or dune-drifted stage:
'Lady Macbeth is houswif full of sin',
'Prince Hel is drinkard tho of nobel berth.'

110 *My Oxford*

> . . . memories of vomiting blindly from
> small Tudor windows (Philip Larkin: *All What Jazz*)

Trinity Term . . . From somewhere down the High
A gramophone enunciates its wish
To put another nickel in, and I
Am going to have drinks with Ernle-Fyshe,
A Merton man who had a poem once
In *Time and Tide*. The future has begun.
Over by Magdalen Bridge the tethered punts
Knock at the jetty. I am having fun.

Upstairs I hand my bottle over, take
A mug of rhubarb-coloured punch, and wave
A sprightly hand at someone. 'I just make
Whatever's made from what you bring.' A grave
Critic from Keble, aged nineteen, says why
The only man is Mauriac. And then
A girl in peasant dirndl, dark and shy,
Asks me to tell her about Origen.

My bow-tie chaste, my waistcoat green brocade,
I lay the law down, and another drink.
Bells clang from colleges, her hair is swayed
By breezes at the open window. Think
How much there is to do (that villanelle,
That *Isis* piece, that essay for A4) . . .
But confidently thinking all is well
I gulp another, sinking to the floor.

Someone recites his latest poem, while
Tom Lehrer's lyrics sidle through the haze.
'What John Crowe Ransom has is purely *style*.'
'Auden is only passing through a phase.'
The girl has turned elsewhere. My head goes round.
Let Mauriac and co. do what they like.
I lean from the embrasure. There's the sound
Of copious liquid drenching someone's bike.

O Golden Age! O Nineteen Fifty-Three,
When the whole world lay wide in front of me!

Your long face, like a camel's, swivels round
The long bar of the George, and stops at me
Coming in like bad news. The BBC
Recruits young graduates to rescue Sound
From all that bright-lit, show-biz sort of stuff
And I am one of them, arrived too late
For the Golden Age (the exact date
October Fifty-Seven), though enough
Remains like a penumbra of great days
To sanctify our efforts. There you stand
Aloof and quizzical, the long bar scanned
For friends or enemies, a scornful phrase
Poised to put down the parasite or bore;
But underneath that mask a lonely man
Looks out, lugubrious comedian
Or elegiac dandy, more and more
Driven into the corners of yourself.
Uncertain of your mood, after an hour
Of a shared office going slowly sour
With cigarettes and hangovers, the shelf
Above your desk capsizing with its load
Of scripts that date back sixteen years or more,
I try the Twickenham ploy, the sort of war
You relish, England–Ireland, worth an ode
Better than J. C. Squire tried long ago.
That does it. You prefer such stuff to bleak
Intensities of bookishness, and speak
With passion of who scored, and how, and know
Each quiddity of form and style and skill.
And yet I play this game only to thaw
That icy stare, because I'm still in awe
Of your most private self, that self you spill
Into the poems you keep locked away.
Looked back on now, how much I must despise
That Boswell-type with deferential eyes

Who saw you as a lion on display!
The living man eluded me. Though praise
Bitten out from those pursed, laconic lips
Astonished me, dismissal could eclipse
My universe for hours, even days.
Now that you're dead, I read you and I hear
Your nasal, almost strangled voice recite
Poems you wrote in loneliness at night,
Far from the George and parasites and beer.
My glum prosaic homage comes too late,
Ten years too late, for your embarrassment,
And yet those truant hours spent and mis-spent
Off Portland Place I humbly dedicate
To a Muse who watches, listens, is aware
Of every sell-out, every careless word,
Each compromise, each syllable that's blurred
With vanity or sloth, and whose blank stare
Chills and unmasks me as yours used to do.
Forgive me, Louis, for such well-meant verse,
Such running-on where you would have been terse,
And take the thanks I meant to give to you.

> . . .born in Lincoln and studied
> at Lincoln School of Art, and
> in London. For a time he worked
> in Paris where he became a friend
> of Toulouse-Lautrec, but in 1904
> he returned to Lincoln to take
> over the family coal merchant business.
> *Note in the Usher Gallery, Lincoln*

Attics and absinthe, girls in shadows
Along the Seine under the gaslight,
And canvas after canvas covered
With botched-up images that hovered
In air for me to get them right
Before those placid flats and meadows
And that safe city on a hill
Beckoned me back again. And still,
Here at the roll-top desk where orders
Are neatly stacked for coke and cob,
Deliveries to Brigg or Bailgate,
The lamps all lit, and working late,
I feel my pulses leap and throb
Remembering art's old disorders.

113 *At the Shrine of Santa Zita**

What are you doing here, quiet under glass,
White frills and flowered chaplet, open mouth
Hard-beaked as a tortoise?
Your leathery hands have done with knitting, baking,
Wiping and dishwashing and mending cast-offs.
You have put your feet up.

Odd at first sight that you should be presented
Thus, like a girl dressed for her confirmation,
Weary of miracles.
Yet the brown mummy spruced so smart and tidy,
Dry skin and bones made housewifely and decent,
Is a true emblem.

Seven hundred years of labour-saving gadgets
Weigh little in the balance put against you,
Gaunt patroness of habit.
It would be pleasant if such daily order,
Such steady working at routines and drudging,
Were always framed so.

Parcelling up the garbage for collection,
We catch the reek of everything neglected
Shoved into corners.
The sweeper-up we do not care to mention
Sets to his chores more ruthlessly than you did,
And sifts no rubbish.

But here you lie in your ridiculous canopy,
An old crone in a little girl's white finery,
Your left hand resting
Restlessly on the lace, as if impatient
To pick a rag up from the floor beside you
And go on dusting.

*patron saint of domestic work, b. 1218, d. 1278, in S. Frediano, Lucca

She tells her grandchildren how her brother went
Off in the ambulance, his big laced boots
Heavy on the stretcher at the ends of legs
So white and thin. A family event,
The prelude to a funeral. She puts
A storyteller's shape on what she says,
And what she says holds them and makes them see
That Yorkshire street, those other, different days.

At nine years old her brother went, when we
Were nowhere, her grandchildren further off
Even than that. An accident, a death.

She pauses suddenly. The unwilled tears come,
She drops her face, and with a little cough
Stops the recital. Round the shadowy room
Children and grandchildren are silent too,
Life standing like a weight we cannot move,
Unmuscled by the thin, sharp shaft of love
That still must wound, and still the wound must show

And all that happened sixty years ago.

The mountain meadow tilted back
Among white rocks and sprawls of berries.
We panted up the mountainside,
Plucking at clumps of grass and pausing
To catch our breath at level places.
And suddenly there, above the meadow,
Through a thin screen of trees, the sky
Exploded with a hundred swallows
Plundering the blue air's farthest reaches,
Threading and stitching side to side
Silently in the silent pasture:
A fuming swirl of wings and bodies,
Violent, disciplined, alien,
A wildness, wilderness, pure and strange.

And vanished then. The empty sky
Ached, and a stunning absence filled
Those lost and vast and cloudless spaces.

Emily's

Tonight we drive back late from talk and supper
Across miles of unlit roads, flat field and fen,
Towards home; but on the way must make a detour
And rescue you from what, half-laughingly,
We think of as your temporary world –
Some group or other, all outlandishly
Named and rigged up in fancy dress and loud
With adolescent grief. Well, we're too old
For alien caperings like that. The road
Runs towards home and habit, milk and bed.

That unborn child I locked up in neat stanzas
Survives in two or three anthologies,
An effigy sealed off from chance or changes.
Now I arrive near midnight, but too early
To claim you seventeen years afterwards:
A darkened auditorium, lit fitfully
By dizzy crimsons, pulsing and fading blues
Through which electric howls and snarled-out words
Isolate you (though only in my eyes)
Sitting among three hundred sprawling bodies.

Your pale face for a second looms up through
The jerking filters, splatterings of colour
As if spawned by the music, red and blue
Over and over – there, your face again,
Not seeing me, not seeing anything,
Distinct and separate, suddenly plain
Among so many others, strangers. Smoke
Lifts as from a winter field, obscuring
All but your face, consuming, as I look,
That child I gave protective rhetoric.

Not just this place, the tribal lights, the passive
Communion of noise and being young,
Not just the strident music which I give
No more than half an ear to; but the sense
Of drifting out into another plane
Beyond the one I move on, and moved once
To bring you into being – that is why
I falter as I call you by your name,
Claim you, as drifting up towards me now
You smile at me, ready for us to go.

Victorian Voices

Here at the bench in front of me, the flasks
Ripple and throb with all the simulacra
Providence has provided; the various tasks
Assigned to each and all by their Creator
Perform and are performed. Forests of spines,
Vitals enclosed in hollow boxes, shells
Built of a thousand pieces, glide along
Majestically over rock and reef.
Yonder a *Medusa* goes, pumping its sluggish way
Laboriously, not ineffectually,
Beneath the surface of the clear wave;
A mass of *Millepore*, a honeycomb
Much like the second stomach of an Ox,
Slimes, reappears, retires, appears once more;
And there, that massive shrub of stone, the coy
Calcareous atoms of the *Madrepore*,
Short branches, branched and branched again, pierced through
With holes innumerable, threaded with tentacles.
Ha! Here is the little architect
Ready to answer for himself; he thrusts his head
And shoulders from his chimney-top, and shouts
His cognomen of *Melicerta ringens*.
Look! He is in the very act of building
Now. Did you see him suddenly
Bow down his head and lay a brick upon
The top of the last course? And now again
He builds another brick; his mould a tiny cup
Below his chin, his sole material
The floating floccose atoms of his refuse. So
Prochronically pellets build to bricks,
Eggs from their chambers, sharks from embryos,
The hollow cones that are the present teeth
Of crocodiles, the tusks of elephants
Refined through layer after layer until
Centuries are accomplished year by year—
And then, after the pulpy fibrous doors
Knocked on in the vegetable world,

The lower tribes, the higher forms – then Man,
Our first progenitor, the primal Head.
What shall we say, we who are chyle and lymph,
Blood, lungs, nails, hair, bones, teeth, phenomena
In the condition of the skeleton
Distinct, the navel corrugated here. . . ?
I ask you this: could God have made these plants,
These animals, this creature that is Man,
Without these retrospective marks? I tell you, no!
A Tree-form without scars limned on its trunk!
A Palm without leaf-bases! Or a Bean
Without a hilum! No laminae
Upon the Tortoise plates! A Carp without
Concentric lines on scales! A Bird that lacks
Feathers! A Mammal without hairs,
Or claws, or teeth, or bones, or blood! A Foetus
With no placenta! In vain, in vain,
These pages, and these ages, if you admit
Such possibilities. That God came down
And made each each, and separately, and whole,
Is manifest in these. Let us suppose
That this, the present year, had been the special
Particular epoch in world history
God had selected as the true beginning,
At his behest, his fiat – what would be
Its state at this Creation? *What exists
Would still appear precisely as it does.*
There would be cities filled with swarms of men;
Houses half-built; castles in ruins; pictures
On artists' easels just sketched in; half-worn
Garments in wardrobes; ships upon the sea;
Marks of birds' footsteps on the mud; the sands
Whitening with skeletons; and human bodies
In burial grounds in stages of decay.
These, and all else, the past, would be found now
Because they are found in the world now, the present age,
Inseparable from the irruption, the one moment
Chosen, the constitution, the condition:
They make it what it has been, will be, is.

The flasks ripple, subside. I am tired. And miles away
I know who sits and writes and tests and proves
Quite other things and other worlds. I fix
My microscope on *Case-fly* and on *Julus*,
The field left clear and undisputed for
The single witness on this other side,
Whose testimony lies before me now:
'In Six Days God Made Heaven and Earth, the Sea,
And All That In Them Is.' Amen. Amen.

118 *A Literary Life*

I tried to open up so many eyes
To the great minds of all humanity.

I thought he liked me, thought I knew him well,
Twin strugglers through the London labyrinth,
Scribblers who learnt the scribbling trade with care –
Though he was never 'Varsity, of course:
How he arrived is something he keeps dark.
A Third in Mods, Second in Law and History,
Is all I have to boast of, but it was
Balliol, with Lang and Mallock, Nettleship,
Prothero, Milner, Rawnsley, Asquith, Cluer . . .
And then my disinheritance (that uncle and his schemes
Of 'business', and my Battels and my cheques,
And mischief in the breach, and no more cheques) –
Well, 'coaching' might have kept me, scraps of Greek
Shoved down the throats of ninnyish nincompoops;
But on that day I strayed into St Giles,
Facing the lectern, opening up the book,
Placing my finger with unopened eyes –
Those words (Acts Nine, Verse Six): 'Arise and go
Into the city, and it shall be told thee
What thou must do.' Nothing in view, alone,
Without inheritance, and penniless,
I came to London.

The 'turnover', my first, a causerie
Of thoughts on 'End of Term' – oh guineas earned
Deliriously, scribbling eight hours a day
Fusty and musty in a dear old garret
Off Temple Bar, addressing envelopes
For half a crown per thousand for the *Globe*;
Letters from Swinburne about Tourneur ('if you should
Run up here sometime may I have the pleasure
Of seeing you in these rooms . . .' – the very words!)
So I aimed high, and higher, up and up –
With Leslie Stephen in the *Cornhill*, Smith
Taking my 'Dryden' for the *Quarterly*,
And work, and work, and work . . . I must jot down this:
That evening, out at Putney, A.C.S.
Invited me to hear him read his new
Volume of poems. Dobson, O'Shaughnessy, Watts,
William Rossetti, Marston – The Pines was full
Of singing birds, and I among them all.
What bliss to see them, hear them, watch the frail
Outlandish Swinburne leap and shriek and moan
Immortal verses! But it could not last.
Another year or so, and we fell out.

Extension Lectures down at Brixton, Richmond
(Frequently honoured by the Princess May,
Later to be our Queen, Duchess of Teck,
And other notables), Hackney (in Lent
Of Ninety-one, 'The poetry of Browning'),
Anerley, Ascot, Balham, Battersea,
Crouch End and Cheshunt, Highbury and Lee –
An interview with Browning, one with Froude,
And then, and then – the Chair at Birmingham . . .

But nothing quite right yet: others made way,
Climbed ladders, set their mark, were darlings all
Of quarterlies and salons and the most
Important colleges – such as my long-time friend,
Or so I thought him, one-time, some-time friend
Who gave those Cambridge lectures – tall and sleek
And full of names dropped, fudge upon the page,
And errors, errors, errors by the ton.
To say so in the *Quarterly Review*
Was – surely? – a good office, what a straight
Purposive fellow ought to say, in truth:
No personal attack – here was a book
(All pasted up for lectures) which was gross
With slovenly facts, deplorable and low . . .
But that I said so – this was beyond the pale,
Though Gladstone, Huxley, Arnold, took my point:
I think they did . . . The truth is hard to find.
What lodges in my skull is that fine phrase
They say the Laureate uttered to my friend
(My one-time friend) – 'You want to hear my view
Of that man J.C.C.? I tell you this –
A louse upon the locks of literature!'

After that, Birmingham, books, and Conan Doyle,
A touch of the old trouble – a low state
Of worn depression, sometimes several days –
And finally, the School of Journalism
To be my final crown . . .

Well, there it was, and here I am, a man
More sinned against than sinning, waking up
At ten to ten in Lowestoft, and going
Out for a walk a little dizzily
(A sleeping draught perhaps), and stepping in
To four foot six of water and thick mud.

Among the many papers found on me
A stained sheet with some careful jottings made
For the forthcoming Johnson Celebrations,
And these words too, which need no note or gloss:
'Poems in couplets written so that each
Couplet has two or three emphatic syllables,
Two or one in the first line, one in the second
Commencing with the same – this is also
The initial of the chief emphatic syllable
In the second line: thus, "I was wearie of wandering
And went me to reste
Under a brod banke
Bi a bourne side." '

And scholarship, and literature, live on:
As once I heeded, heedless others stray
Ennobled in their errors. Here I lie.

119   *To a Girl of the Period*

Will the bent bow spring back, the strained cord break?
Will temperament and long usage prove too strong?
But three months married, and I ask how long
All this will last . . . Before him, other men
Seemed apt to take me gladly: I refused,
Notoriously unanchored, a free woman
Convinced that all society is built up
By process of experiment, that the last
Word has not been said on anything.
These were the very phrases that I used,
Intent to build the future with a past
Weighed, sieved, rejected if the test so proved.

*

And was it then for pity that I loved,
Or thought I loved? Those boys and girls of his,
Quaint scoffed-at relics, an eccentric's toys –
All dressed in coarse blue flannel, Nazarenes
With love-locks to their shoulders, picturesque
As Botticelli's angels. One forgave
Thoughts of unfitness for their beauty's sake –
And so their father: his face the face of Christ,
Believing revolution was at hand,
When wars would cease, when justice without flaw
And abstract right would swiftly take the place
Of mere expedience, when the reign of peace
And truth and purity of life – alike
For men and women – would begin at last.

So I have walked the wood, and have picked up
The crooked stick. But wherein lay the flaw,
As it still lies? For he was sweet in word,
His manner acquiescent, and he smiled
To be compliant – indeed, did much I wished
Because I wished it. But I never touched
The core. The shortcomings, the weaknesses,
Lay all about. The intimacy of marriage
Forced them upon me.

               We kept open house –
But open to our opposites: round him,
Poor patriots and penniless propagandists,
While those whom I invited he pronounced
'Worldly, ungodly, frivolous, fashionable'.
For him, my taste in proper sense of dress
(Off with the children's medieval rags
And on with frocks for girls, jackets for boys)
Was dandyism, forethought was faithlessness,
Conventional propriety just 'fashion'.

Was it my money ruined us, dependence
Of the traditional breadwinner on one
Who added to her faults of practical rigour
The graver fault of riches? His engraving
Brought in its fees, but was precarious.
The burden of the children and the home
Fell to my energies, while Utopia
Took all his time. Clean linen tablecloths,
The accurate adding-up of butchers' bills,
Were trivial stuff to him – and to me also,
Yet must be seen to. All my early ardour,
The independence which I sought and won,
Reduced to coaxing, nagging, silences
More terrible than either . . . Well, the parting came,
So gradual that *drifting* is the word
That fits it best.

                    And words are what I have –
Use, now, as my sole weapon – not to call to arms
The Shrieking Sisterhood, Wild Women shrill,
Revolting daughters (as experience
Lived through and suffered might have given me cause),
But to *condemn* them, sexless masks of men,
Hard, without love, ambitious, mercenary,
Without domestic faculty and devoid
Of healthy natural instincts . . . So with spitting rage
Women and men attack me, 'Girl of the Period'
Cartooned and comedied and turned to farce,
The hoyden travesty. No one in the world
Honours and loves true women more than I,
But then they must be *women* – with their faults,
But better than the adopted faults of *men*!
Misrepresented and misunderstood,
I pen another article while I know
Its fate is to be twisted, jeered at, burnt,
Mangled for sermons, told it takes a view
Branding a woman no better than a cow . . .

★

Maternity – that blessèd, blessèd word
Fulfilling womankind, its benisons
Denied to me. With scarcely hidden tears
I tell you that this little rush of Fame,
This famous notoriety, is nothing
Compared with that imagined ecstasy
For which I yearned, for which I was so fitted
By temperament, by body, and by skill.
Babes of my reveries, shawled plumply in my arms,
Products of finest art, of care and love,
You must belong to others. Knowing all
In my own person, all that women suffer
When actively they launch into the fray,
I would prevent with all my strength young girls
From following my own unwilled mistakes –
Guard them, indeed, with my own body from
Such insults as my life has given me,
Teach them to be themselves – and to be free.

120 *Messages from Government House*

The Punjab war is done: in all the land
No man in arms against us. Those who bolted
Ran through the Khyber Pass and go on running.
They came like thieves and dash away like thieves.
The Maharajah and the Council signed
Submission yesterday, the British colours
Were hoisted on the Citadel of Lahore,
The Koh-i-noor surrendered to our Queen,
And the Punjab – each inch of it – proclaimed
A portion of our Empire. What I have done
Is my responsibility. I know it
Just, politic, and necessary; my conscience
Tells me the work is one I pray that God
May bless; and with tranquillity I await
My country's sanction and my Queen's approval.

It is not every day an officer
Adds to the British Empire such a prize—
Four million subjects, and the priceless jewel
Of Mogul Emperors to his Sovereign's crown.
This I have done—but do not think that I
Exult unduly: I do not. But when
I feel conviction honestly that this deed
Is for the glory of my land, the honour
Of her most noble majesty, the good
Of those whom I have brought under her rule,
Fitly I may indulge a sentiment
Of honourable pride. Glory to God
For what has been achieved.

                Some other matters:
A curious discovery at Rangoon—
Digging an old pagoda to make way
For army barracks, our men came across
Gold images and bracelets, with a scroll
Showing these things were put there by a queen
Five hundred years ago. In all such places
One or more images are found of Buddha:
Our fellows call them 'Tommies'. There are few
Pagodas to be seen without a hole
Made by ingenious Britons in their search
For Tommies. I am sorry to admit—
Accessory after the fact, you know—
I purchased secretly myself some bits
Of this mythology when first I reached
Burmah.

            I have a sad death to report—
Bold as his sword, high-minded, kindly, pure,
Devoted to his calling, Mountain is gone.
A Christian soldier, died as he lived. He rests
In the old cemetery at Futteghur.
His widow's on her way here; he'll go home
By the next steamer.

                    I have just received
A packet of the rhododendron seeds
Despatched from Kooloo, which the Duchess wished,
And trust they will do well.

                    The troops have driven
Moung Goung Gyee out of the Irawaddi:
They took him in the jungle – took his gong,
His gold umbrella and his wife. A pity
The man himself escaped. The place is quiet.

From Barrackpore to Simla, from Peshawar
To Kunawar and Chini, from the camp
At Umritsur to Attok, there is peace.
The reinforcements from Madras have come,
So now I calculate 14,000 men
(5,000 Europeans) are there, thirteen
Steamers upon the river, besides marines
And many sailors. Opium stands high –
On each *per mensem* sale the Government
Gains well. The punishment we meted out
To Rani and to Bunnoo is rewarded –
The Rani people whom Sir Colin thrashed
Last May, destroying valley, stoup and roup,
Have just come in with turbans in their hands
Begging forgiveness, offering allegiance,
Submitting to our fortress. Our success
In sowing dissension between tribe and tribe,
'Twixt Mussulman and Sikh, Hindoo and all,
Is clear: suspicion reigns, and union
Is hopeless between any. Peace and plenty!

                    ★

Just as the office mail was going out,
A rising in Bengal among the hills –
Barbarous folk, though usually timid,
Armed just with bows and arrows: some say greed,
Some say fanaticism, some ill-treatment
By those who build the railway. Troops are there
And closing in. The trouble has not spread
And soon should be put down. But what vexation
Just at the close of my career . . .

*

Before I lay this sceptre down, I plan
To show the court in a most frank despatch
What has been done in India these eight years –
And left undone. I look things in the face.
'Opus exegi': taking leave of those
I ruled over, tomorrow I embark.
The Friend of India some months ago
Called me 'not personally popular'.
If that is true – 'tis not for me to say –
Never were full and copious tears so shed
Over a man *unpopular*, wiped away
By bearded men . . .

                I am quite done; my leg
Gives pain continually. Let Canning do
The best he can: the brightest jewel of all
In our imperial crown weighs heavily.
Less easy every day the burden lies –
Annex one province, two others will rise up
Like hydra-headed monsters, their partition
A parturition. What will be born of this?
Rumours and panics and religious wrath
At a few cartridges . . . and 'hope deferred'
At Delhi, given time, indeed one day
'Makes the heart sick' in England. Blow away
The rebels from our cannons, still there hangs
A cloud of blood above the hills and vales,
Ganges, and Indus, and my lost domains.

156

Alfred is visiting the Misses Trigg,
Devout old souls whose thread is almost cut;
The girls are at their tasks; and so am I,
A careful mother whose peculiar care's
An infant's pure delight in little things.

O Observation – though restricted now
To Ecclesfield, this room, these walls, this bed –
How I have used you, for diviner use!

In parables and emblems all things spell
Lessons for all of us – my humble gift.
Every true story of humanity
Contains a moral, wrapped and neatly tied
Like an unopened parcel for a child.
We are all children in the eyes of God.
The Crab, the Starfish, and the Bird of night,
The valiant Oak, the Robin Redbreast – all
Teach the inquiring infant to accept
Things as they are, in equanimity.
Red Snow, they say, that falls upon the Alps
(Though I have never ventured from these shores)
Or Great Sea Tangle such as Columbus saw –
Of these I am cognisant, but am more inclined
To nearer things, to close domestic signs.
See how the Bee plunges within the cup,
Fretting its legs with nectar, golden dust,
Always industrious, sweetly employed.
The Long-tailed Tit (*Parus caudatus*), I chose
After a passage by the Reverend Johns
(*British Birds in their Haunts*) – a happy choice
To illustrate 'the happy family':
For from the moment that a young brood leaves
The nest until next mating season comes,
Papa, Mama and children keep together
In perfect harmony – the same tree-clump

Is their society, they choose together
The next place they shall flit, no one disposed
To stay when all depart, molesting no one,
And suffering, as far as one can see,
No persecution. Here is a pattern made
For all young hands to copy.

                                    It is true
Nature has crueller ways: the House Spider,
Having secured her web, constructs below
Hidden from view a silk apartment whence
Threads are extended, forming a cunning bridge
To the rayed centre – out, then, rushes she
Like a small thunderbolt, seizing her prey with fangs
Which suck the victim dry of all its juices
And then casts out the skeleton-remains!
I do not dwell on that. The value of hair
As a manure for rose-trees was told me
By a prizewinning gentleman who gave
Credit for his success to this device:
Dig in a sheltered place, go pretty deep,
Place in the hole a bone or two, some hair,
Water with soap-suds – practical advice,
And interesting too, to indicate
Animal assisting vegetable,
As vegetable does likewise in its turn.
Nothing can be more satisfactory
As to results. Neither our confidence
Nor yet our comfort are misplaced; no fear
Of being taken in; in all such matters
We are not at chance's mercy; everything
Goes on with regularity, by rules,
By habit; or, as naturalists word it,
By virtue of some *Law*, firm, definite,
A stringent fixity, the Light of Truth.
It is a will on which we can rely;
From past expressions of it, we presume
The future; so we rightfully say *Law*.

The Dragon-fly Grub – a creature whose appearance
Is most unprepossessing, and whose character
Is hardly amiable – can be kept
Happily in a foot-pan filled with water
And fed from ponds or ditches with live insects.
Observe at leisure Metamorphosis –
How, at the chosen moment, this vile thing
Climbs up the Flag or Iris planted there
For your experiment – a rent appears
Within the Pupa case, the wings expand,
And the winged tyrant of the airy world
Most beautifully ascends.

                  O read the book
God's servant, Nature, puts within your ken!
There in these works which seem to puzzle reason
Something divine is hidden, to be discovered
By patient scrutiny. Thus, crickets sing
Loudly, and most troublingly by day,
In damp conditions – as in a cottage here
Where a young mother died by slow degrees
Of a consumption; and it seemed as though
The crickets heralded the sad event.
See on my sun-dial the words I chose,
Hallowed by constant observation – 'Watch,
For ye know not the hour . . .'

                  Now, Juliana,
The day's dictation's finished. Kindly copy
My words in your fair hand. My own, disabled,
Aching and helpless must lie here unused
Upon the counterpane. I have employment,
I see the sun, love life. And when you pray,
Pray not that I may have less pain but that
More patience may be mine.

Hockley is turning Papist, so they say:
His set is stiff with incense, and he bobs
Most roguishly in chapel. More and more
The Whore of Babylon extends her sway.
Branston is fiddling with his 'little jobs',
Copying the Bursar's buttery accounts
Into a pocket book he locks away.
In Common Room each night, the floor
Is held by Foxton, face flushed like a plum
About to drop – and we have seen him drop
Drunk as a carter in the smouldering grate.
They are all here, my *Corpus Asinorum*,
Donkeys in orders, stuffed in jowl and crop.
One day it will be said 'He did the state
Some service', when they read my book of fools.

The Master's slack. He does not know the rules.
He is – can't be denied – a natural curate
And would be better suited to the cure
Of souls in Wiltshire, ministering to pigs.
I've seen old Figgins watch him like a ferret,
For Figgins was passed over, and for sure
Preferment went because Enthusiasts
Clamoured for someone without Roman views.
But – pardon me – the Master strokes and frigs
His conscience like a trollop with an itch
Flat on her back and panting in the stews.
All pious mush dressed up as manliness,
Evangelistic canting, keen to bring
Trousers to niggers who don't wear a stitch.
A man's religion is his own. To sing
Barnstorming stanzas to the Lord's as poor
As Newman fluting eunuch fancyings,
His heavenly choir on earth. O that old Whore,
How devious she becomes!

                                        This elm-smoke stings
My eyes at night, when I should be holed up
Snugly behind the bulwark of my oak.
Some more Marsala, or another cup
Of punch . . . What frowsty collared priest is this,
Another chum of Kingston's on the soak
Or snivelling gaitered surrogate from Bath?
Give me your arm—I needs must go and piss.

My colleagues all tread down the primrose path
That—who?—oh, Shakespeare then—put in a play.
I should be even now, I tell you, hard
Pent in my room and working at my book,
Theocritus, my text, my elegiac
Pagan . . .

                    How these chatterers swill and stay!
I'll take a turn with you around the yard,
The farther quad where dotards never look,
Or if they do, then always back and back
To the dark backward and abysm of time . . .
But then we all are backward-lookers here,
If you would understand me: relicts, men
Who hear the echo when we hear the chime,
As Great Tom stuns the silence. In my ear
I sense the falter of the tolling bell,
I hear it boom again, again, again,
Fetching me back and back, not boding well,
And the full moon hangs high across St Ebbe's . . .

Where was I? Morbid, maybe, at this hour
When Master, Bursar, Chaplain, Dean and all
Waddle like corpulent spiders in their webs
To winding staircases and narrow beds,
To livings without life, posts without power,
A benefice without a benefit.
I have you all marked down . . .

Later he wrote: 'On 24th September
Shocked to hear of tragic death of friend
&c': 'keen regret' to him long after
That I and she to whom he was attached
So warmly 'never met or were acquainted
And now would never . . .'

            He was more astute –
Though no less given to subterfuge – than I,
Who saw him first a young, raw, fresh-faced thing.
The 'attachment' that he wrote of was but one
Melded with many others – love-longings
He used as I could not.

            My longings led
Down to the back room of the *Lamb & Flag* –
Brandy-and-water till the dreams took over,
Wafting me back to times when all ran right,
All was about to be, nothing came sour
Against the throat and tongue, nothing looked dark
Against the study-lamp . . . But then the raging,
The boasts and incoherences, the tags
Bellowed or muttered to an audience
That played me for its sport, a thrashing minnow
Swelled to a pike and gorging on the hook.
And, at the last, a brother's troubled arm
Helping me up and out and home to bed,
To toss and twitch and, sweating, sleep it off
Till the next bout would have me in its grip.

The miseries we have become compounded
By those we guess are yet to come, the failings
That magnify to failures. First the sighing
Winds that portend a shower, the scattered drops,
The downpour venting to a steady drizzle
Drenching before and after. So it was:

Small gifts that proved yet smaller, all ambition
Shrunk to a modicum, a way of life.
Workhouse accounts inspected, another novel
Judiciously dissected in review,
A reputation coddled till it smothered.

Onset of autumn – melancholy time
In Cambridge, mists uprising from Coe Fen
Over the causeway, Michaelmas daisies drenched
Drooping their heads in college gardens. Shrouds
Gathered on candles, and foretold a death:
Whose death was supposition – but I knew,
Even as by the mantelpiece I stood
And talked, and heard them guttering; and he
Recognized, too, the sign. And all such signs
Were his to play with, twists and turning points
For fictions, symbols, circumstantial plots . . .

If she I fumbled in hot madness knew
How things had fallen out, our issue growing
Monstrous, strung up as witness of our sin
Though long estranged, the dire inheritance
Of evil warps, repugnant origins,
She would be privy to them. And she knew –
Because she had to bear – the sad beginnings.
I – we – and our son too – we have been used
By one to whom I was mentor . . . yes, and friend:
The dutiful recorder of my trust,
Advice, remonstrance, love. What Homer said,
What Virgil took through labyrinths of metre,
What all my lavished learning broke and spilt,
He bore away, and stored, and deviously
Set out in his inventions. Meanwhile I
Drudged here and there, perpetual ordinand
Not fit to be ordained, my weaknesses
Disguised as scruples or as personal quirks
Familiar to familiars.

                              Yet I loved him
As one untainted by my shameful spells,
As one fit to be fledged – and then he flew!
How far and with what difficulty flew,
Far out beyond me, beyond that grey day
Far from our Dorset heath, our ambulations
Entranced with all my nurturings of talent,
Beyond the too-entrancing Cambridge courts
I lapsed towards, seeking again a brother. . . !

Dear brother in the outer room, you hear
A kind of trickling, a sound you cannot place:
That cold commemorator I encouraged
Will place it, use it, all grist for his mill.
I took the open razor to my throat.

Old pupil, you have new material now.

124 *A Message from Her*

(*Modern Love*, v)

I

So I dissembled: you dissembled too,
Striving to gain the fame you could not have.
You thought me your importunate young slave.
I thought you fierce to attain the things that you,
You only, could achieve. So we were wrong
In feigning each was only bent on each,
Eyes signalling to eyes, not needing speech.
The labour hence was tortuous and long,
Words broke to sentences, each phrase strung out
Like drunken men striving to stretch their thirst
Into the dawn, or lovers who at first
Believe each touch and kiss a final bout,
And then renewed, renewed . . . And each goes on
Battling, and feinting, reeling under blows
That deaden as the deadly feeling grows
That they are dead indeed; and dead and gone.

II

That gentle painter with beseeching eyes –
He was no menace: not the first, at least.
Some other bore the sign, mark of the beast,
Before he ever came. What sad surprise
When I escaped – more matter for your art!
This was the dizzy sickening of your will,
Sisyphus labouring up the stony hill,
Something that drained the nerves and pierced the heart:
An emptiness that gave me room to breathe
But vacuum to you – and how you strove,
Your lungs protesting, with what you used to love,
Your murderess . . . So our passions seethe,
Spill over, settle, chill. We learn to die
By living our own lives, leaving a room
Furnished like any self-respecting tomb,
The funeral bands disguising vacancy.

III

I left a note: 'He is in tears – I must
Go to him now.' And so the hours went by,
And you, of course, knew I could never lie.
But there I lay, lapped in an alien lust
That you could never understand, nor ever
Satisfy. Those broodings, those inert
And silent pangs that shadowed your sad hurt,
How could you contemplate what came to sever
Mismatched endurances with such a blow?
My love – my once love – you were far away,
Remembering some distant hallowed day
When from my gown I let the loose bands go
And I was Princess to your wandering Prince,
And all was fable, Land of Faery . . .
What you cast out, what you could never see –
That was the simple truth, long vanished since.

IV

No word of me in letters, never a word
Let fall from that point onwards that I shared
Eight years with you, or that I ever cared
Concerning you. Fled like a migrant bird
To climes unknown, in ignorance I became
A footnote to your *opus*, quite cast out
Like the lean scapegoat who must bear the doubt
Because no other creature bears the blame.
And so I sickened – pitiless endless pain,
The swellings and the achings. Pale and weak,
I stumbled into debt, wrote letters, bleak
Day after day. For you, the deadly strain
Was not *my* dying but *your* distant fear
Of sickness and of death. I knew I must
Face on my own the test, accept the just
Reward for sin, and nowhere seek a tear.

V

How strange to be remembered in this way!
A set of almost–sonnets, crabbed yet rich,
Abrupt yet ample, stitch woven into stitch
As line by line you tell the present day
What happened, who kept silent, which one spoke
Words that must wound, how reverie went wrong,
And each verse carrying its bitter song –
Bitter, reproaching nothing but the yoke
That kept us bound together. This is how
Art will remember us, not in the ways
That stretched and broke us through those racking days
But in the mode that's apt and modish now:
Art for Art's sake . . . Forsaken, you set down
A set of tablets permanent as stone.
I was a wisp, a nothing, on my own,
Commemorated with an iron crown.

You think I'm drunk because my Irish voice
Is thick and crapulous – ah, there's a word
You wouldn't give me credit for: you think
I'm thick as peat, sir, thick as two short planks,
Because you hear my stumbling bumbling throat
Expectorate a load of roughened vowels.
Why smoothness, sir? Why should I learn to trim
Words that are mine to suit the vocables
That, polished, come from *your* mouth? I imbibed
Fine terms and cadences from all my tribe,
The Irish minstrelsy.

                         A crippled beggar
For forty years, a beggar before that
Since I could walk – my mother turned me out
To beg, because my father served the crown
In Egypt or some other foreign part
And never came back. I learned no trade. I might
Have learnt the shoemaking, but what's the use?
Fine times I had when the French war was on –
I lived in Westminster, one of two hundred
We called the Pye-Street Beggars, and our captain
Was Copenhagen Jack. Jack's word was law.
Each day he formed us up, gave us our beat:
'Twas share and share alike – the captain extra.
We had our lays – oh yes – the 'blind dodge darkies'
Who played at being blind, 'shakers' with fits,
And shipwrecked mariners who'd never seen the sea,
And men who took a bit of glass to scrape
Their feet until the blood ran – dodging lame, sir . . .

Not like my honest lameness. A horse and cart
Drove over me – well, yes, a trifle drunk, sir.
We lived like lords with Copenhagen Jack –
Fifty'd sit down to a supper, geese
And turkeys and all that, and keep it up
Till daylight with our songs and toasts.

                                    Oh no,
There's nothing like it now: the new police
And this Mendicity Society has spoiled it all.
When Jack was 'pressed, his boys got rid of me –
They skinned me, took my coat and boots, turned out
In tatters on the 'orphan lay'. I cried
All day on the doorsteps, with my captain gone.
That won me ha'pence, though, and silver too,
And when I brought the swag home all the lads
Danced round and swore they'd make me captain next.
But when they'd had their fun, they took it all,
Kicked me under the table. I ran away,
Found a new house – St Giles – no captain there,
But better treatment. A hundred beggars,
Two or three hundred more in houses near –
Now all those houses gone, sir, taken down
When Oxford Street, New Oxford, was built up.
Oh we lived well then, St Giles and Westminster –
Eight, ten, fifteen, aye, thirty shillings a day
I've earned a-begging.

                              Not one shilling now.
The folks don't give today as they did then,
They think we're all impostures. And the police –
They won't let you alone. No, sir, I told you –
I never knew aught else but begging work:
How could I? 'Twas the trade I was brought up to.
A man must follow his trade. No doubt I'll die
A beggar, and the parish'll bury me.

A rum, sir? Thank you. And I'll speak you such
A ballad as my forebears left to me
From Holy Ireland. No, not drunk at all –
'Tis but my speech, a cockney Irish yet
The inheritance of kings, of bards, of saints,
Crippled, on crutches, with a tray of laces.

Pale beauties of a former day, lie there
Suppliant slaves attentive to my gaze!
My brush must worship you, large-eyed, bereft
Of all but wisps of gauze and feathered fans
In such a heat, the ancient classic sea
Glimpsed blue through the embrasure. How you strain
Mutely at these constraints I put on you,
Languid on couches, supine by the pool!

How different the view as now I turn
And look on dank back-gardens, dripping walls,
Façades of terraces, a distant spire,
And rank on rank of villas sprawling up
To crown this city fate has given me . . .
If I had been brought up among your groves,
Your temples and your chambers, purple-draped,
Sun-drenched in marble, what might I have been!

And so I use you, distant and ideal,
Maidens of modesty, passionate and still,
To be my paragons. My purposes
Are chaste, exact, sublime, and beautiful,
However men may misinterpret such
Voluptuous offerings – the upraised breasts,
The yearning thighs, the lips that, swollen, speak
Impulses we deny except to Art . . .

Back to the canvas . . . Think – in Manchester
My allegories grace those blackened fanes,
Suggesting a perspective we have spurned
In votes, and bills of lading, and machines
That knit and fret and petulantly stamp
Patterns on shoddiness, an endless wheel
Of usefulness and profit. Yet my shapes –
Lovingly nurtured, individual . . .

They say I make my profits too. 'Tis so –
I tug the heart, the lost inheritance,
And so the purse-strings. Is that shameful, then?
To please with what would else be lost to us?
They speak of *markets*: I am fortunate
In doing best what's best for my design,
Romantic ardour in a classic vein,
The pristine captured and brought down from heaven.

Watch how I mix the umber with the rose,
Tinctures of flesh beyond imaginings,
The dew still on the petal, light of light,
Waterdrops glistening on the lifted arm –
A talent, and a gift: no muddiness,
No crudity, no vaulting after vague
Resemblances, but everywhere my crisp
Edges of excellence, a bounding line.

These Frenchmen and these Dutch – I've heard of them,
But what about them? Vogues will come and go
As they have always done. The test must be
Standards established by the chosen few
Time has preserved for us – Praxiteles,
Phidias, a handful else. Where can Art go
Except in emulation? Here – the pink
Lies on the white, and trembles on the cheek.

Rich bronzes, figured vases, jewellery –
Fruits of my labours, subterranean joys:
My men sit round a dark sarcophagus,
Broken and plundered centuries ago,
And nod at noon. I sift and sift again,
Under the hottest sun, in longest hours
Of sleepy sweltering heat, intent on each
Small shovelful of soil, or sand, or ash.
No matter that the London functionaries
Hold back my proper monies, ignoring letters,
Museum men walled up in bills of lading,
Idly content that yet another consul
Should now and then transmit them treasures. Mine's
A nose for all that's oldest, finest, rarest,
From shy Etruscans to these desert shores
Where Battus first made landfall and the light
Of Greece first dawned in darkest Africa.
White-crowned Cyrene – never have I seen
A Grecian city so commanding, high
On its acropolis, with all around
A wilderness of tombs, deep lintelled caves,
Domes, and hog-backs, and noble architraves,
And hoarded grave-goods (even though despoilt
By brigands old and new) that catch the breath.

Not so this post my lords have given me –
A dreary town stuck betwixt sea and sand,
Salt-lakes, and hovels windowless and low
With stable-yard interiors like middens,
A crumbling castle, one poor minaret,
One grove of date palms, line after line of walls
Monotonously red, the houses unhewn stone
Bedded in mud, and rain, and filth, the whole
Wretched confusion a barbarity
Fit for the Barbary Shore . . . A tail-less lion
Over my doorway, in as quaint a style

As Mycenean, and a flag-staff—these
Alone distinguish my abode as **that**
Which represents Her Majesty. I hope
I am not doomed to a long exile here
In this *Ulubrae*, sand-girt, dead-dog-strewn.
Smyrna, Palermo—those I covet most . . .

Still, for the present I must grant it has
Greater attraction than it would possess
For many people: diggings established, soon
I hope to make a good haul of antiques.
As for my consular duties, I have borne
In mind your last injunction, that I should
Ingratiate myself among the Arabs. The other day
I visited a powerful tribe in camp—
Five or six hundred horsemen at a gallop,
Brandishing their long rifles, shouted welcome
And honoured me with races, firing muskets.
I am on good terms, also, with the Pasha:
I stood firm to his claims, and he withdrew
Pretentious interferences. I begin
To understand these oriental gentlemen—
I wish I could claim as much for what I know
Of their outlandish languages . . .

                              Many tombs,
Well-furnished I would guess, are even here
Hard by Benghazi, on the salt-lake shore.
More to the north-east, on the Tocra track,
Relieve the barren undulating waste,
Unfreshened by flower or shrub, by leaf or blade.
It is of these I wrote at the beginning,
The Tocra vases, finely beautiful,
Panathenaic some of them. Even more
The port of Apollonia presents
Far richer prizes, if I can persuade
A *firman* from the Pasha. Where I fear
Sole opposition is from the Brotherhoods,

The Convents of Senoussy who keep up
Fanaticism and intolerance
Among the lower Arabs: dangerous men.
Twice in my tour they threatened me with talk
Of 'Nazarene dog', and at Ptolmeita I
Escaped only because my *exequatur*
Displayed the Sultan's signature. Such trials
Do not, however, bring me to despair;
A spice of danger lends a certain relish
To searching for antiquities.

        If Lord Somers
Should be inclined to pay this coast a visit,
I would delight to be his *cicerone*. Did I mention
At Apollonia the numerous columns
Of cipollino, relics of Christian churches,
To which the Turks attach no value, but
Which I am sure would be much prized in England,
Either perhaps to adorn the National Gallery
Or decorate the portico of a church?
May I beg the Admiral at Malta to allow
Some gunboat, on a cruise, to bear me hence
And lift these handsome spoils? Such prospects lighten
The burden of this wretchedness, the whines
Of Maltese litigants, the silences
I long endure from London. My dear Sir,
I beg you not to let me languish here,
Though I am avid for what treasures yet
May be vouchsafed to me.

Can these thick-pelted Calibans, deep in their dripping forests,
Be human as I am, or else collateral
Ancestors, the kin of apes and monkeys?
Such questions exercise the gentle reader
Snug in his study, holding in his armchair
My books of travel: they are not my questions.
Journeying, I best follow the old author –
Humani nil a me alienum puto.
For, from the moment England drops behind me
With all its rules of upbringing and habit,
Sensible tracts, quotidian drudgeries,
And all my dismal memories of girlhood,
I grow another face, become another person.

Travellers, indeed, are privileged to do
The most improper things imagined with
Perfect propriety. The sickly elder daughter
Whose youth was spent reclining on the sofas
In rectory drawing-rooms, with spinal trouble
That nagged through camomile and laudanum,
Now jolts on horseback through the wilderness,
Land of the Rising Sun's most northern island.

Evenings in plaited huts, gulping down rancid stews
(Boar offal, spongy roots, unnameable victuals),
Saké libations to the million deities
Worshipped in mountain, tree and rock and river,
Dim-lit interiors where elders endlessly
Spell out the genealogies of tribe and tribe,
And over all the mystery and the deluge
Descending like a revelation on me.
For God is here, among these (you say) savages,
As instrumental in his signs and wonders
As anywhere in tamer, temperate places.
No, I do not presume the evangelical:
My part is not the preaching of the Gospel,

Though some could only gauge what I am doing
In terms of carrying Bibles to the natives –
Aunt Mary as a missionary in India
Or Cousin Mary among Persian deserts.
These Ainu have no written law or history –
Indeed, no forms of written words among them –
And, placid in their sad, sweet resignation,
Only inflamed by copious potations
Of rice-wine spirits, are uncomprehending
At notions of a Saviour among them.

If you cast doubt upon the seemly wisdom
Of trusting female frailty to the dangers
Exposed by such benighted sole encounters,
I ask you, reader, merely to examine
Your storyteller as she stands before you:
Four-foot-eleven, a stumpy dumpy creature,
At her age – rising fifty – unencumbered
With fancies how her charms might be like tinder.
I trust myself to Ito, my interpreter –
Sharp-witted, vain and bandy-legged, a youth
Hot for his girls, his sweetmeats and his pride.
A foreign lady capable of 'drinking
To the gods' in their intoxicated fashion
Without intoxication, and whose questionings
Seek out the best and not the worst in all men –
They cannot harm me. Diligent and merry,
The grooms who take my horses and are humble
Could not depend entirely on the tardy
And insufficient efforts of the niggard
And selfish Church I grew in and grew up to.
God numbers these in his inheritance:
These heathens puzzled by the word 'salvation'
Will yet be saved – but not by my endeavours.
The gates of Heaven are wide and full of mercy,
Opening to all who follow in their fashion
The instincts they may never have acknowledged,
Whether Hawaii, Arkansas or Yorkshire
(Parishes known or unknown, known to me),
Loosed them to make their world their destiny.

Peevish I may be, briefly, at my portion
(I should have been a man, though would not say it
Except to Ito, who'll not understand),
But this I know – accept – embrace – and glory in –
The freedom of a journey that excuses
All things but cowardice, bad faith, incompetence,
And leaves me free to look at what was never
Revealed before to the sick English daughter
Of a good man who never could envisage
The stumbling trackways she can now exult in,
Far from the rooms she lay in once, alone.

129   *The Potter's Field*

Here, sir, a fine display of bravery
And fortitude, all rendered out of clay –
Here's Caius Mutius holding his right hand
Within the fire, showing Porsenna
The firmness of the Roman character;
On the reverse, the maid Cloelia
Selecting from the youthful hostages
Whom Porsenna will liberate. A piece
Noble and highly wrought, you will agree.
And by this vase, a terracotta plaque
Depicting in relief Da Vinci's great
'Battle of the Standard' – lavished round the rim
Oak leaves and acorns in the classic style.
This modelled wall-hanging won Second Prize
In 'Eighty-two at Braintree – Lucilus
Personates Brutus, an Old Master's work
Young Edward copied with a master's skill.
Glazed ornamental is our special pride,
Gem-ware encrusted, sprigged and polychrome –
But we love precedent in everything,
Old lessons handed on, the apostles' touch
Rendering all we make a sacrament

Blessed by the past – Egyptian, Roman, Greek,
Palissy plates and Babylonian shapes,
These ewers after Orazia Fontana's,
Tazzas adapted from Fijian ware
(Queen Emma of the Sandwich Isles came here,
And shook me by the hand, and bought a fine
Large model of our castle-keep, the source
Of so much inspiration – solid stuff,
Impregnable though ruined). Even these
Humbler creations have their ancestry:
Barm-pots and costrels, benisons and cloams,
Pottles and salt-kits, gallipots and tygs,
The rude plain earthenware, traditional instruments
Rustic amusement used, the puzzle-jugs,
The bird-whistles – I made them, one by one
And gross by gross, to stock the waggonloads
That left our workshop, sagging above wheels
Bedded in mud, for markets dwindling down
To half a dozen hawkers raucously
Shouting our old-style wares to new-style ears . . .

For that I fear's my story. What I put
In stone above the lintel is my text –
The psalmist's strong stern voice: 'Except the Lord
Do build the house, they labour in vain that build it' –
And vain the labour too. With sweating kilns
That marred whole bungs at firing, bubbles, bloats
Scarring the intricate sprays and sprigs and lugs,
Added to muddle casting-up accounts,
And sons who emigrated or who died,
And Fashion sniggering at our 'quaintnesses',
Grown fond of delicate mincing porcelain . . .
Fine feathering, tib-work, the antique ornate
Crossed with the sturdy native English style,
Slumped to mere jobbery, plain coarse flower-pots,
Nothings by anyone for anyone,
No individual stamp, no sense of that
Grandeur I gave a title to – 'Unique
Art Pottery Works of Castle Hedingham'
('The *Royal* Art', after Queen Emma's visit).

Zion bewails her pitiful estate,
'Esteemed as earthen pitchers' – meaning held
As low as dirt.

               And yet our dirt is *clay*,
Grog, slurry to be fashioned into lives
As vivid as the mud our Infant Lord
Shaped into sparrows from the gutter-side . . .

                                  ★

The grunting drays convey the crocks away
Where they will gather dust in crumbling sheds,
Back-ends of warehouses, a bankrupt's stock.
Here in my cottage by the castle wall
I slowly foot the treadle of the wheel
That turns the last ceramic I shall make
Before the vessel's broken and the sherds
Are thrown on to the spoil-heap where we lie
Until the angels' golden trumpets sound,
The Master Potter works his mystery,
And every fragment to its fragment's joined.

A dozen dogs, poodles and nondescripts,
My darlings barking at the iron gate . . .
Who might it be? There's no one left to call,
And so I sit useless, the garden wall
High as my disappointment, sit and wait
For the moths to eat away the innocence,
The honesty, the decency, and then
The whole new wardrobe I could not afford
From Worth – the vanity, the vain expense,
The flirting with Marchese and with Lord,
The opinionated converse with true men.

Now Robert Lytton's dead – a heart attack –
And della Stufa – cancer of the throat –
And Mario, too, whose voice enslaved me once –
All loves, all friendships, straitened and remote
As former fame, and flower-filled hotel rooms,
The Langham thirty years ago . . . Look askance,
You moralists who jib at genius,
At the pert message posted in the hall –
'Leave morals and umbrellas at the door.'
No invitation to reception, dance,
Wine, *conversazione*, concert, play,
For – what? – a dozen years . . . A villa, dank
And crumbling among cypresses, four floors,
Twenty-five rooms – myself and Gori stay
When Bagni drifts with leaves, and all have left.
Condemned to solitude, in poverty,
Furniture seized by creditors, bereft
Even of letters bundled over years,
Manuscripts auctioned, each royalty and fee
Reduced to farthings . . . No, these are not tears
But the dulled liquids of blue eyes that saw
Irving perform my gestures and my words.
Out of the world, my world, perhaps so much
The better, walled up here midst dogs and trees –

I am old, pathetic, angry, out of touch.
The world takes its revenge on us, because
We once despised it. Play it as you please,
Rewards must dwindle, style must go awry,
Voluptuousness grow vile, and Europe learn
The rage for slaughter. Middle-class spirits crush
The rapture and the passion of the soul,
Making it mute: thus Browning, Tennyson,
George Eliot—in chains, or chanting odes,
Or hypocritical in homilies.
Our genius is our spur, our passion goads
The highest from the best. Even in the tomb
The lustre shines like gold from sepulchres
Of lost Etruscan kings, or on the breast
Of some fair living woman, undimmed by dust,
The length of ages, or men's pettiness.

*

My dogs bark on among the cypress gloom,
A dozen Cerberuses whose yelps press
Hotly against the neglected effigy—
My own—where like a Florentine princess
I lie in Bagni, dead, unread, my name
A half-romantic joke, something to see
If tourists can be bothered to search out
A deaf custodian with a rusty key.
No flowers, no candles, no *frisson*-laden words
Await you there: the candles have gone out,
The flowers have faded, and the words are dull
As out-of-fashion dusty ballroom clothes
Hanging in wardrobes in deserted rooms.
The iron bell-handle's broken: when you pull,
The dogs grow hoarse not at the sound of it
But at the unfamiliar, painful smell
Which men call Life. And I am out of it.

Uncollected Poems

Damp logs, foul spitting planks,
A smoky pile of still unseasoned timbers –
The river sniffs and pushes at its banks,
Remembering the embers
We hauled from its turbulence and tried to burn.
Now it is our turn
To feel that loss, to be punished for our pains
As a stinging cloud billows out and stains
Ceiling and walls, prickling our eyes
With half-dead fumes, resinous memories.

These bits we cannot burn – lumber
Not to be consumed, reduced to ash –
Fill the shared room with odours, and encumber
Our lungs with dross, with trash.
What is combustible goes quite away
And will not stay
To simmer, splutter, blanketing the place
With reeking sullenness we cannot face.
Let them lie long, dry out, forget the river,
Ignite and flare and drop away forever.

The surfaces of earth – all rigid now
Wherever mud hardens or branches brace
Their strength against the hoar-frost as its lace
Drenches in stiffly whitened mists – show how
Things keep their postures as an accident,
Were never meant
To be seen *now* or *now*, a moment caught,
Frozen, recorded in an eyelid's shutter.
A pheasant rises, brilliant, in a flutter
Of skirling bronzes, noisily distraught,
Wrecking the field's composure.
Everything falls back startled, disarrayed,
Begins to flow again; after that brief exposure
Resumes a world that can't be stopped or stayed.

133 *The Stump*

The mower hits it, screeches, sheers away:
No more than half an inch of surfaced wood
Bedded in grass, each year seems to be dead,
Lopped with an axe by someone on some day
Before we bought the place. What sort of tree
I can't begin to guess, so little's left
As, year by year and cut by cut, the shaft
Prods up, is sliced, reduced, until I see
Nothing except a disc flush with the earth.
Dead, surely. Till in summer, mowing there,
The blade tears round it, screaming, giving birth
And being aborted, as the growing year
Refuses to forget what once grew there.

134 *What Animal*

What animal is this, so safe and cared for,
Cosseted even, with his mate and young
Trustingly by him, comfort and room to breathe,
Nourishment guaranteed, secure among
Refreshments such as spirit and body crave for—
Why, then, does he seethe
Resentfully, stare at the far horizon
As if bars blocked his way, making a cage
Where no cage is? What walls enclose his prison?
A futile aching rage
Seems to bow down his head and fix his teeth
Wretchedly in his own well pampered flesh,
Nuzzling to touch the bone buried beneath,
To start afresh
Wounds healed and mended, convalescent sores.
What animal? Such questioning ignores
The trail of trodden footprints to this place,
The old familiar smell, the placid stream
Running so clear and slow you see your face
Reflected, as with the sharpness of a dream
You know the creature, know the cage is yours

Though there is neither cage, nor walls, nor bars.

135 *The Bed*

Facing the head of the bed, a stranger would see
Always you on the right, me on the left:
Your pillow higher, softer, mine no more
Than a thin ridge tilting my sleeping head
Above the horizontal. Your body curled,
A question-mark, a foetus: mine hulled down
Prone, legs straddled, left hand flung above.

Habits of night, when bodies meet and touch.

Reach for the bedside lamp and put it out.
A hand exploring, two hands moving over
Familiar surfaces. The tender ache, the comfort.
Each knows the other's places like a face
Daily encountered in the bathroom mirror.

Also, at times, the tears, the silences,
Bad dreams before sleep comes, and absences
Waking to shrill alarms' routineless clamour,
With you alone, as I have been alone,
Elsewhere, waking to stare at shattered patterns,
Feeling the sun come up in other rooms.

The cold bit of the bed no bodies touch.

136   *Dream Time*

Waking from a bad dream, and thrashing out
So that you too woke, and I heard you say
'What is it, love?' – why, at my sudden shout,
Did I pretend more stirs, more mutterings,
A kind of baleful play,
And knew I left you with sad wonderings?

Was it because the dream that made me speak
Excluded you, close though you were to me
And are? For each one's dreaming is unique:
Rejected here and there we lie alone,
Separate, distinct, free,
Each one's heart as heavy as a stone.

137 *Waiting*

All day the telephone in silence sits.
We are forgotten. The whole sky is blank.

I read a Kurdish poem: 'Nothing sadder
In early morning than to see stooped workmen
Building prisons'.
                              This is where we live,
Envied for what we have, for what they think we have.

Love isolates and binds, puts up its walls.
We are inviolate. The air is still.

From dawn till bedtime, nothing.
Jangle of keys beyond the outer gate.
Promises simmering, a lifetime's pause
High on the brink.
                              Whatever lies below
Covers its wings, folds over, falls asleep.
The telephone in curtained darkness sits.

138 *Now and Then*

How difficult *now* is:
Then silts up, spills over
With unstoppable memories,
Or – if to come – is a hill
In the distance under a cover
Of cloud, unseeable
And yet predictable.

Now is the point of the pen
Making a single mark
And hurrying on, till *then*

Is the whole page covered,
Or the page covered tomorrow
After the passing dark,
The plough passing over the furrow.

139 *To a Manichee*

In a dozen different ways
All of them the same
You tell us life is terrible

You tell us with crushing of bones
You tell us with rending of sinews
You tell us with boiling of blood
With the man degutting the woman
With the woman decapitating the man
With the ant devouring leviathan
With the wren dissecting the octopus
With the wolf drooling over the lamb

And all this while
Someone called God is there
Doing nothing about it

So it goes on
So it goes on

Till another book hits the shelves
With a noise like thunder
With a sound like applause
With a high cry of approbation.

And life goes on just the same
Terrible terrible
The whisper of terrible despair
Comforting the comfortable.

140   *The Small Brown Nun*

The small brown nun in the corner seat
Smiles out of her wimple and out of her window
Through thick round glasses and through the glass,
And her wimple is white and her habit neat
And whatever she thinks she does not show
As the train jerks on and the low fields pass.

The beer is warm and the train is late
And smoke floats out of the carriage window.
Crosswords are puzzled and papers read,
But the nun, as smooth as a just-washed plate,
Does nothing at all but smile as we go,
As if she listened to something said,

Not here, or beyond, or out in the night,
A close old friend with a gentle joke
Telling her something through the window
Inside her head, all neat and right
And snug as the white bound round the yolk
Of a small brown egg in a nest in the snow.

141   *Indian Images*

Lutyens' red sandstone stands and lords it still
Over the laid-out placid capital,
Far from white oxen ploughing, where a boy
Follows behind to catch the falling dung,
To bake it dry for burning; far away
The poison lodged beneath the cobra's tongue,
The plaintive voice entreating you to stay.

Happy the dancing mango-breasted girls,
Happier the fondled gods embraced by them.
Clay on the potter's wheel spins out, unfurls,
And the black lingam, sticky at its stem,

Renews the fertile world; while down the road
A charpoy bears a shroud, no follower,
No family. At railway-halts, 'Stop Dead'.

Earth wears, and earthenwares – a child's whipped top
Slowing and tilting. In the barley-pot
A mongoose; on the slopes, Golconda's fall.
Red fort, white mausoleum, beautiful
The insolent vulture wheeling over all.
Insects' monotonous bleep; a steady flood
Blessing the roads with betel and the fields with blood.

142   *For Frank Coe*
(1907–1980)

Drinking cold beer with my uncle in Peking
Night after night that cold and windy spring
(And he was dying then, and is dead now),
He told me in his pinched exhaustion how,
When the Red Guards went crazy, it was Mao
Held back the mob and let them live in peace:
The compound by the Drum Tower, the small trees
Ruth planted and watered, shelves of pots and scrolls,
All safe against the furious tide that rolls
Towards the things it envies.
                                        You survived
Burnings, jail, purges. So the 'new age' thrived,
And in your lungs the cancer too. Your room
Stifled because your body froze. The bloom
Touched the first branches of the peach: out there
A million bicycles swerved and clanged, unaware
Of all your years in exile, renegade
And refugee, wry dignity that stayed
Even as in your pain you joked and drank.
Strange relic from my childhood, when I thank
Your kindness and your love, I must thank too
The inscrutable caprice that granted you
That end in your walled garden that cold spring
And the first peach buds blossomed in Peking.

The world exploded: ash and atoms both.
But it was not 'the world': only Japan,
And only part of that. It was a myth.
Under the myth, people once more began
To crawl through ashes, wreckage, poverty.
The fumes subsided. The volcano's breath
Exhaled on the horizon.
                              Stand here, see
This tiny spider chancing its puny death
On mud that bubbles half an inch below.
Coke-tins and plastic judder in the pool,
Boiling and rising.
                              Spring Festival; and so
The affluent crowds (young ones with *Cool, Man, Cool*
On sweatshirts) mill about, spill out from cars,
Enjoy the blossom, holiday, rich peace.
Try *Sexy Carnival*. There are no wars:
Only the TV Space War stuff. *The Police*
Throb from transistors, transliterated *Pax
Nipponica*. The red sun is unfurled.

Across the western sea, a billion backs
Bend to the four trends, lug the turning world.

At the edge of the world is a very neat castle
In miniature, owned by the National Trust.
It is possible to rent it on a weekly basis,
Briefly enjoying neo-gothic illusions
As one gazes west through narrow-leaded windows
On terminal rocks assaulted by fierce seas.

Like a chess-piece isolated in an extreme situation,
This rented folly is a thing to play with.
Among simple and tasteful furnishings, a plain table
Carries a drawerful of journals with consecutive entries
By previous temporary tenants, praising the amenities,
Suggesting pubs, recommending itineraries.

But stranded awkwardly among all these pages
One entry is different: evidently by a woman,
Taking the place on her own, beginning like the others
With observations of birds, of walks, of weather,
It modulates gradually to tell of encounters
With a strange man polishing a scythe, of finding a stone

Inscribed with obscure words, of dreams about witches.
The handwriting degenerates, syntax goes incoherent,
Lurid obsessions spill over. Then, abruptly, it stops.
Perhaps she was playing at fiction, putting on a style
Suitable for a week in a neo-gothic folly.
But, having read it, my mind has not been easy

Here at the edge of the world in this very neat castle.

145 *At the Flood*

He comes by the window, or I think he does.
The river is up, the water close to the door.
Will he reach the field beyond us, and come back
Saying the bridge is dangerous? Will I go out
And guide him with a torch, trying myself
With careful footfalls, showing him it's safe?

He is at the door. It is dark, and the water laps
The fence a yard away. Will I ask him in,
Give him a bed, acknowledging the bridge
Is now one with the river, can't be crossed?
Will he take advice, or trust himself, or will
The river, rising, answer for us both?

He has knocked. I open to him, speak, and take
The torch out in the dark. We reach the bridge.
The water covers it: I show the way.
He goes across, the field is now a lake,
The far field takes him in. I turn and go
Back to the lit house. And the rain comes down.

146 *In the Gravel Pit*

In the steady rain, in June,
In the gravel pit by the pylon,
This empty afternoon
Walking there in a dead
Mood, I found one
Not caught inside my head.
Caught quite otherwise,
What was a rabbit, just,
Crouched with its blank eyes
In a sodden lump of fur
In grey indeterminate mist.

It did not even stir
As I stood there in the rain.
Mud-trickles down the bank
Oozed under its paws. What pain
It felt I do not know.
The gravel pit had the stink
Of wet silage, of the slow
Decay of thrown-out stuff.
And as I stood and watched
This end of a scrap of life,
I did what I had to do.
For the first time, it twitched
As I stooped and set my hand to
A broken plank in the mud.
I struck maybe seven times,
Till its eyes burst, and its blood
Covered its wretched fur,
And no sound, no whimpers or screams,
Only my own roar
Of misery, ignorance, pain,
Alone in the gravel pit
By the pylon in the rain,
And my hand with its own blood
Torn by a nail that bit
As I struck at a dead mood
And an animal dying there
Without meaning in the mud
In the warm summer air,
With the rain still soaking the earth,
And everywhere, in the blood,
The dying, the giving birth.

Profiles. Some sharp, some worn; some bright, some dull.
Coveted, shut away, now brought to light.
Forty-five years ago, trays heaped and full
Were spread for my inspection as I knelt
High on the Leeds shop stool and took my pick.
It was of history they felt and smelt:
I lingered over them.

                Now, quick
And furtive, almost, as if fingering dirt,
I pluck them out, confront the expert's stare.
He squinnies at them, mutters, asks what's fair,
What I expected, what they'd fetch. So, hurt
Or just resigned, I let him name a price.

Forty-five years ago, each was a trophy, each
Saturday sixpence snared another catch –
A William or a Charles, farthing or groat,
Rubbed Roman bronze (silver was far too much),
Devices puzzled over, dates deciphered,
My father looking on, helping me read
Blunted inscriptions, emblematic coat,
Or lurking mint-mark.

                Later, shut away,
They waited to be sold off till today,
An attic windfall picked in middle age.
The cost of things, inflation rising fast,
And bills to pay and mouths to feed, or just
A weariness at so much bunged-up past . . .
I see his bits of paper, glad to have them.
(So much sour verdigris, corrosion, wear
Among the bright and sharp ones. So much dust
Gathering in attics, never put to use.
What would I want them for, why should I save them?)

'Thank you, in cash.' The past is an excuse.
Achievement; shame; blankness; relief; disgust.

Insect remains extracted from a sample
represent a 'death assemblage'; their
bodies have come to lie together in the
archaeological deposit, but there is no
proof that in life there was any connection
between the groups.

> From *The Analysis of Archaeological*
> *Insect Assemblages: A New Approach*,
> by H. K. Kenward.

They huddle together,
Heads, trunks, limbs – see,
Rigid in ashfall,
Blasted in fusion,
At the end of their tether,
Solid but flimsy.
At this long interval
In time's deposit
There must be confusion
Whether their exit
Brought them together,
In semblance of unity
Assembled, or whether
In life they were separate.

Disaster-theory,
Archaic but possible,
Assigns them a date
Which (in old reckoning)
Is quite conceivable
As late nineteen-hundreds.
But no true connecting
Of body with body
(And so many, so many)
Can ever be ventured.

149 *Afterwards*

Look at it now: a country drugged with language,
Familiar streets and houses with their posters
Stripped from the walls and windows, the dead echoes
Of rhetoric still lingering on the air,
Prolonged in chat-shows and in interviews.
Exhausted faces grey in newspapers,
Poets reading to embarrassed sniggers,
The sound turned down, the vision flickering.

So for the jeremiads, the post-mortems,
The letters-columns stiff with rectitudes.

I can't believe all this. I'm feigning anger,
Or disillusion, or the end of things.
My little world is not made cunningly,
And yet it's made, has lasted until now.

150 *At Evening*

They were always there, at the end of the garden or elsewhere
Talking unfathomably about whatever it was
In a way that even in childhood I could understand
Enough, at any rate, to feel frightened of.
And here they all are again, as I stoop to brush off
Four or five grey hairs from the arm of the chair – still talking,
Their heads close together, familiar faces in congress,
Knowing I'm there, not afraid to talk when I'm there,
But secret too, surreptitious. I wish I could hear.
The shadows move down the garden, the bonfire smoke
Drifts across hedges, the smell of the smoke pricks my nose,
The hairs on my arm stand up as evening comes on:
And still they are talking, talking, and I want to go in,
Into the house where I know I have always been.

151 *Soseki*

(London: December 1901)

A lost dog slinking through a pack of wolves.

Sour yellow droplets frozen on each branch,
The tainted breath of winter in the fog:
Coal-smells, and cooking-smells (meat-fat, stewed-fish),
And smells of horse-dung steaming in the streets:
Smoke groping at the windowpanes, a stain
Left hanging by the mean lamp where I trace
Page after page of Craig's distempered notes . . .

> Winter withering
> Autumn's last scattering leaves:
> London is falling.

I want a theory, a science with firm rules
Plotting the truth objectively through all these infinite spaces.
I look out of the window over the whitened blankness,
And from the Eastern Mountains the moon lights up half the
    river.

But it is hallucination: cab-lights from Clapham Common
Flash at the pane, my head throbs over the little fire,
I am crying in the darkness, my cheeks sticky with tears.
Far, far beyond the heavens the forms of departing clouds . . .

Downstairs, those sisters plot and scheme together –
I found the penny on the windowsill,
The one I gave the beggar yesterday. Ridiculous pity,
Sly instruments of torture!
                            'Soseki's mad' –
That telegram sent home by Okakura –
Will they believe it? Is it so? Is he my friend?
I have no friends. By the light of the dying fire
I underscore these lines, and more, and more . . .

December evening.
Light at the window shining.
Something in hiding.

London is districts learned from Baedeker
And learned on foot. England is somewhere else.
A day in Cambridge seeing Doctor Andrews,
The Dean of Pembroke, offering me sherry.
Too many 'gentlemen'–at Oxford too.
Someone said *Edinburgh*, but the speech up there
Is northern dialect, Hokkaido-style.
So London it must be–the Tower, its walls
Scrawled with the dying words of men condemned;
Lodgings in Gower Street with Mrs Knot;
That vast Museum piled with pallid Greeks;
West Hampstead, and then Camberwell New Road . . .
I measure out the metres as I walk,
Finding sad poetry in the names of places.

Sometimes, walking the streets thronged with such tall and
     handsome ones,
I see a dwarf approaching, his face sweaty–and then
I know it for my own reflection, cast back from a shop-window.
I laugh, it laughs. 'Yellow races'–how appropriate.

'Least poor Chinese'–I think I hear–or 'Handsome Jap' . . .
Sneers of a group of labourers, seeing me go by
In frock-coat, top-hat, parody of 'English gentleman'
Sauntering down King's Parade or in the High . . .
I walk to Bloomsbury, walk back to Clapham,
Carrying my Meredith or my Gosse through the drizzle,
Munching with difficulty a 'sandwich' on a bench in the park
Soaked by the rain, buffeted by the wind . . .

Far, far beyond the heavens the forms of departing clouds,
And in the wind the sound of falling leaves.

It is time to be deliberate, to use
Such gifts as I am given, to escape
The traveller's to-and-fro, the flow of facts
Unchecked, to make a system that will join

Blossom to branch, reason to intuition,
Wave after wave uniting as each falls
Under the next that follows up the beach . . .

A cry outside shakes
The tangle of waterpipes:
Midnight: a mouse squeaks.

A frightened mouse in a cell facing north,
I have almost forgotten what brought me here
Or what I do from day to day.
                                I know
I sat with Craig for an hour this morning,
Hearing him mumbling Shakespeare through his beard,
And gave him seven shillings in an envelope
Bound round with ribbon which he plucked away
Impatiently and mannerless – due fee
For pedagogic drudgery. So walked back,
Wondering could I afford a mess of eggs
In the cabby-shelter out in Battersea,
And settled for a farthing bun and 'tea'
Scabby with milk served in a cracked white mug
At the stall by Wandsworth Bridge. Such humdrum things
To maze the mind and clog the intellect . . .

By the old castle at Komoro
The clouds are white and the wanderer grieves.

Impenetrable people, country bumpkins,
Nincompoop monkeys, good-for-nothing
Ashen-faced puppets – yes, it's natural
Westerners should despise us. They don't know
Japan, nor are they interested. Even if
We should deserve their knowledge and respect,
There would be neither – because they have no time
To know us, eyes to see us . . . Lesser breeds:
We need *improvement* (Brett has told me so),
And Western intermarriage would improve us.
We are the end of something, on the edge.

The loneliness, the grieving heart of things,
The emptiness, the solving fate that brings
An answer to the question all men ask,
Solution to the twister and the task.

'Tears welling up in a strange land,
I watch the sun set in the sea':
Yes, true, but for the sun, which once a week
May sidle itself weakly through pale clouds,
And for the sea, which somewhere – south or east –
Lies far beyond me, and is not my sea.
But tears well up, indeed, in a strange land
And speak of nothing but my lack of speech.
Curt monosyllables jab and jabber on,
Perverted versions of the tongue I know
Or thought I knew – the language Shakespeare spoke,
And Samuel Johnson's sonorous clauses mouthed
By me, alone, in Kanda, Matsuyama,
In Kumamoto . . . sailing through such seas
And on such seas of rhetoric and doubt
Towards these other islands where the sun
Has set before it rises, Ultima Thule,
Where tears well up and freeze on every branch.

I creep into my bed. I hear the wolves.